T0159054

BUILDING
RELATIONSHIPS
ONE CONVERSATION
AT A TIME

BUILDING
RELATIONSHIPS
ONE CONVERSATION
AT A TIME

A Guide for Work and Home

CAROL ANN LLOYD-STANGER

BUILDING RELATIONSHIPS ONE CONVERSATION AT A TIME A GUIDE FOR WORK AND HOME

iUniverse books may be ordered through booksellers or by contacting:

iUniverse
1663 Liberty Drive
Bloomington, IN 47403
www.iuniverse.com
1-800-Authors (1-800-288-4677)

ISBN: 978-1-5320-3193-9 (sc)
ISBN: 978-1-5320-3192-2 (e)

Library of Congress Control Number: 2017913503

Print information available on the last page.

iUniverse rev. date: 01/09/2018

For my mother, who taught me how to build wonderful relationships with meaningful conversations

CONTENTS

Preface ix

Introduction: Relationships and Conversations........................ xi

Chapter 1   Making Relationships a Top Priority 1

The Impact of Relationships.. 1

The Extended Reach of Relationships 4

Stories and Storytelling... 6

Building Blocks of Personal and Professional Connections.... 11

The Success That Matters Most.. 18

Chapter 2   Choosing the Best Conversations to Have 21

The Power of Choice 21

To Have or Not to Have 24

Perspective 25

Direction and Alternate Routes... 31

Outcomes and Destinations... 34

Chapter 3   Listening and Understanding Your Way to Success.... 43

Time to Learn... 44

What People Want... 46

To Build a Bridge.. 48

Questions That Get Answers.. 52

Listening Builds Relationships 58

Chapter 4 Exploring Style and Making Connections 61
      Image and Expressions 62
      Why People Don't Get You 64
      "It's Just the Way I Am" 65
      Style, Substance, and Setbacks 69
      Ways Style Can Work for You 74

Chapter 5 Solving Problems and Creating Solutions 79
      Hallmarks of Tough Conversations 79
      Out of the Frying Pan 82
      Tough Talk with Yourself 84
      The Path to a Better Outcome 86

Conclusion: Getting Started 103

Notes 111
Index 115

PREFACE

No road is long with good company.
—Turkish proverb

Our lives are shaped by relationships. Friends and family members, colleagues and neighbors, even competitors—all these people and our relationships with them contribute to some of the most meaningful moments of our lives. Those relationships are started and nurtured through great conversations. In years of working in youth and adult education, years of developing and presenting workshops about professional communication, and years of working with individuals seeking to experience greater personal and professional success, I've learned three important things:

1. People make the most progress when they seek the success that matters most to them.
2. Most people associate success with the people and the important relationships in their lives.
3. The greatest tool we have for building strong personal and professional relationships is conversation.

A client shared the example of how a simple conversation started a long-lasting, important relationship. While in a high school physical education class, my client started running required laps around the gym. Someone ran up to her and asked, "Can I run with you?" Simple question. My client said yes, and a friendship began. They started with what people often call small talk: other classes, favorite teachers, interests, siblings, and parents. Small talk isn't really small; it is foundational. Later conversations covered the same material in more important ways: favorite classes became career plans, interests became life plans, and family members created new relationships. Conversations built relationships that supported these women through the years.

People sometimes ask me why I choose to focus on conversations. In all the work I've done over the years, the big decisions, big successes, and big ideas all happened because of conversations. Conversations are how we share our lives. When people define success for themselves, it includes other people. Personal and professional success depends on relationships. And relationships depend on conversations. Big conversations and small conversations and everything in between.

Also, I'm a big Shakespeare fan. After all, Shakespeare is still a best-selling author, and his plays are still produced all over the world—four hundred years after his death. We all know the stories and characters he created more than four hundred years ago. We use words and phrases he taught us more than four hundred years ago. Shakespeare created characters and stories and language patterns that have lasted for more than four hundred years. And he did all that through conversations. Shakespeare used conversations to create the worlds he wanted.

We can do the same thing. We can have conversations that create our worlds. We can have conversations that build the personal and professional relationships that create success. The possibilities are endless.

You can live the life you want to live—one conversation at a time.

RELATIONSHIPS AND CONVERSATIONS

Friendship is born at that moment when one person says to
another, "What! You too? I thought I was the only one."
—C. S. Lewis

This book is a guide to focusing on the relationships that make our
lives meaningful. To keep relationships strong and growing—and
start new relationships that contribute to our growth and the growth
of others—we need to have nurturing, healing, encouraging, and
fun conversations. We build relationships one conversation at a time.

We live our lives through our relationships. As children, we
learn to navigate the world through relationships with parents and
caregivers. Then we gain a sense of self as we establish relationships
with other children. We go to school and have opportunities there to
establish relationships with teachers, other adults, and more children.
As life goes on, we exercise more choice in our relationships. We
meet new people, get to know them, and determine whether they
are a good fit for us in our lives.

Our relationships matter because they have almost unlimited
potential to bring us joy and sorrow. When we are in positive,
meaningful relationships, we are happy and healthy; when we are

in destructive relationships or are isolated, we are less happy and less healthy.

In addition to gaining benefits from relationships, we can provide benefits to others. We support friends and family members, sharing their worries and their successes. We strengthen communities as we volunteer our time and talents, share our resources, and spend time listening to others. We become part of something larger than ourselves through our relationships.

To a significant degree, relationships make us who we are. The quality of our relationships has an impact on our physical and emotional health, our academic and professional success, and the growth and strength of the organizations we work for and the communities where we live.

Relationships shape our personal and professional experiences. Our relationships can bring us happiness, increase our effectiveness at work, improve our health, and extend our influence through our communities. Building positive relationships can help us define success and allow us to create the lives we want.

We create and strengthen relationships through conversations. Conversations are the way we learn about other people, share ideas, and solve problems. Any conversation with a stranger might turn into a great friendship. Any conversation with a colleague might uncover a great new idea that will turn a business around. Any conversation with a neighbor might inspire you to make positive changes for your neighborhood. Any conversation has the potential to be a game changer. And any conversation can be the one that makes all the difference in your relationship. The right conversation can change everything.

My mom never missed a chance to meet someone new, get to know someone better, encourage someone to grow, or reassure someone that everything would work out for the best. She never missed a chance to have a conversation.

Choose to say hello, to ask interesting questions, to listen more than you speak, to believe in what's possible, and to make meaningful connections.

You can build better, stronger, happier, more wonderful relationships in every area of your life—one conversation at a time!

People are lonely because they build walls instead of bridges.
—Joseph F. Newton

CHAPTER 1

MAKING RELATIONSHIPS A TOP PRIORITY

Lots of people want to ride with you in the limo,
but what you want is someone who will take the
bus with you when the limo breaks down.
—Oprah Winfrey

The Impact of Relationships

Meaningful Relationships Make a Difference to Physical Health

Studies show that relationships have a direct, lasting impact on our physical health. Although doctors and researchers don't know exactly why, there is consistent evidence that people who are in meaningful relationships are physically healthier than people who are not.[1]

People who feel isolated report much lower satisfaction with personal health than those who have positive relationships. Individuals who feel isolated report struggles with depression and high blood pressure. Doctors have noted a correlation between loneliness and the dysregulation of immune systems. In other words, the lack of social connections is related to an increased chance of illness. In addition, without the support of friends, people who are isolated suffer from more stress and associated health problems.

Developing and maintaining meaningful relationships might be thought of as a matter of the heart—and that turns out to be physically true. People who have positive relationships have fewer heart problems and lower instances of heart-related deaths than people who don't have these relationships. Relationships also have an impact on less serious health problems—for example, people with healthy relationships have fewer colds.[2]

The benefits of positive relationships include improved physical health from childhood and teen years through old age. Researchers at the University of North Carolina at Chapel Hill found that the quality of social ties affects various health factors. The researchers found that in addition to healthy diet and exercise, an active social life and connections with other people are essential for good physical health. Developing a strong social network, then, is an inexpensive way to develop better health over a lifetime.[3]

Meaningful Relationships Have a Positive Impact on Mental Health

Experts have found that individuals who have positive relationships experience benefits to their mental and emotional health.[4]

A recent study of cancer patients shows that those patients who had fewer satisfying social connections had higher levels of fatigue and depression. For the patients in the study, the effects of feeling isolated proved to be long lasting. The researchers found that patients who expressed loneliness were afflicted with higher blood pressure even years later.

On the other hand, patients in the study who had strong social connections experienced faster recovery. Positive relationships made patients feel that they were supported and cared for. Those feelings of support and care resulted in patients having less stress and depression, even in the face of serious illness.[5]

Positive relationships are also associated with higher self-esteem. This better sense of self frequently results in greater personal growth and especially feelings that one is able to meet challenges. In fact, social support can make challenges seem less daunting. A group of researchers assessed whether social support had an impact on the perceived difficulty of a task. Researchers placed heavy backpacks on University of Virginia students and asked them to stand at the base of the hill and estimate how difficult it would be to climb. Students who were with a friend and reported having strong, close relationships gave low estimates of the hill's steepness and difficulty. Those who came alone and reported having few or no relationships thought the hill was very steep and would be very difficult to climb. One conclusion of the study was that friendship changes the way we perceive the world.[6]

Positive relationships are also associated with people feeling more confident and more satisfied with their lives. Meaningful relationships help people cope with feelings of depression, anxiety, and anger. Feeling the support of others, people are able to move past these negative feelings. Strong social networks lead to people feeling happier about their lives.[7]

Positive Relationships Contribute to Academic and Professional Success

A strong social support system is a key indicator of student success. Students who develop relationships with teachers and other students do better in school. Joining a group of students who are successful in school can have positive academic and social benefits for individual students. Students who make friends with high-performing students adopt some of their attributes and behaviors and earn higher grades themselves.[8]

The association of a strong social network with success extends beyond school into the workplace. Professionals who develop positive relationships at work report greater job satisfaction and happiness at work. Sales professionals who have positive relationships make more sales.

People who develop close friendships at work are less likely to leave their jobs. They are more engaged with the entire organization, and they are more engaged with other employees.[9] They continue to develop skills and be recognized for good work, and they are more productive with their work tasks. This translates into commitment to the organization and connection to the organization's success. These employees perform higher-quality work and achieve more. They also get higher-level jobs and earn higher salaries.[10]

As most professionals spend the majority of their waking hours during the week at work, having positive work relationships makes their lives more enjoyable overall. People who develop meaningful relationships and friendships at work report feeling better about their work lives and their lives in general.

The Extended Reach of Relationships

Positive Relationships Influence Organizational and Community Success

Having positive relationships with coworkers and supervisors contributes to employee engagement, which provides benefits to the organization as a whole.

Higher morale and greater job satisfaction ultimately lead to lower levels of employee attrition. Organizations that have a positive environment are able to attract and keep top employees. This ability to retain talented employees will result in reduced costs and increased profits for the organization.

Employees who have meaningful relationships are better team members. Working with others successfully, these employees are committed to each other and the organization. They demonstrate their commitment by going the extra mile. These are the employees who will make extraordinary efforts to further the organization's success, and the commitment of these employees spreads within their work network.

Employees who are able to create good, strong relationships with their customers are rewarded with more sales and repeat sales. Customers who trust individual employees trust the organizations those employees represent. This translates to lower costs and higher profits for organizations.[11] The rewarding effects of these work relationships extend into the community, as positive talk and recommendations from customers provide great opportunities for organizations to promote their business to new customers. Positive relationships among employees and with customers lead to higher annual growth.[12]

Relationships can also have a positive impact on communities. In Roseto, Pennsylvania, members of the town experienced only half the rate of heart disease death as did people in the surrounding communities. The people in the other towns were similar to the people of Roseto in race, income level, age, and eating habits. What made such a difference in the health of the people in Roseto? They had extraordinarily close family and community relationships. Despite a diet that would not be considered healthy by experts, the close-knit community created an atmosphere that consisted of high levels of happiness and low levels of stress. Researchers found that this trend held from 1955 until 1965. As time went on and social ties were dismantled, the heart disease rate became the same as that in surrounding towns. The loss of the sense of community and family support in Roseto seems to have contributed directly to the increased incidence of death from heart disease among its population. Losing community and family support has serious consequences.[13]

The Journal of Applied Psychology assessed the significance of relationships and a sense of community. Based on this study, an article in *The Atlantic* considered two siblings: a brother who had left the small town they grew up in to pursue his academic and professional ambitions and a sister who had stayed in the town, cultivating relationships and raising her family. When the sister became ill, her brother returned to help her and was struck by the amount of support she had from her community. He remarked, "It took a village to care for my sick sister." Watching his sister's experience, he found that the "good life" consisted of being grateful. "That's what she did, which is why I think she was so happy … Community means more than many of us realize." Ultimately he moved back to the small town and the community that were full of such meaningful relationships for him.[14]

Stories and Storytelling

We Have Conversations Based on the Stories We Create

The brother in the *Atlantic* article reimagined his story when he decided to leave his "successful" life to return to his hometown. We all have large and small stories in our lives. In fact, every day we create stories to make sense of our lives. We typically do this without even realizing it.

Let's say one morning, a neighbor walks by you without saying hello. Usually Tom says hello when he walks his dog past your house while you're loading up the car and getting ready to head out. But today, he just walked by. Later, when you think about this, you make up a story.

Wow. I wonder why Tom didn't say hello. I bet that dog of his left a little something on my yard and Tom didn't bother to clean it up. That's why he hurried by without saying anything. I am so sick and tired of people not cleaning up after their pets. I can't wait until I get home tonight. I'm going to march right over there and give Tom a piece of my mind.

So, based on that story, you confront Tom that evening and have an unpleasant conversation.

On the other hand, let's say you create a different story.

Wow. I wonder why Tom didn't say hello. Maybe he's worried about something. I remember him saying something about his mother being sick. I hope she's not worse. Tom must be really worried. I'll pop over there after work to let him know I'm available if he needs anything.

That story would lead to a very different conversation.

What we know about other people is almost never the whole story. We fill in the gaps. We turn partial stories into more complete ones, adding our own details to make sense of a situation or behavior we don't understand. We then use these stories as a basis for conversation.

Considering the various ways we tell stories will help us understand the narratives that surround us.

"Report" and "Rapport" Conversations

Linguist Deborah Tannen describes two different types of conversations: "report" and "rapport" conversations. Report conversations are conversations that are focused on information exchange, on getting facts from one person to another. Rapport conversations are conversations that are focused on developing connections and intimacy with another person. Report conversations are transactional. Rapport conversations are relational.[15]

Do you need to know the time and place of a community meeting? Have a report conversation. Do you need to know the percentage of increased sales over the last six months? Have a report conversation. Do you need to tell your staff that insurance forms are due by noon next Tuesday? Have a report conversation. Report conversations can easily be managed via email or a very brief conversation.

Do you need to understand why your teenage daughter is so worried about her history project? You need more than a report—you need a relationship. You need your daughter to trust you and be able to tell you what's really going on. Do you need to understand why an employee is late to the staff meeting every Thursday? Something is going on with him. If you want to understand what it is, you need more than a report. You need trust and understanding. You need rapport. You need a relationship. Have a rapport conversation. Focus on ways of increasing understanding and making connections. Build a relationship.

Many conversations have report and rapport components. Both information and a relationship are at play. Both are important. Both are necessary. Several parents have shared the following example with me: A child goes off to college and calls home. The father (according to my friends) asks the report questions: budget, class schedule, meals. The mother asks rapport questions: getting along with the roommate, feelings about being away from home, loneliness or homesickness, potential new friends. Of course, this isn't true of all parents, nor is it a statement on gender parenting; it's just an observation from a bunch of my friends (and from my own family).

All the information is important, and there's no need to pass value judgments on it. But it is helpful to be aware that different conversations will have different goals. When my mom called, she had some interest in what I was doing at work and how my new car was running and what books I was reading for my book group. But she was more interested in just talking than she was in those particular topics of conversation. "I love hearing your voice, whatever you are saying," she would say. The content was less important than the connection. Other people who call might be more interested in the specifics, in how well that car is running. And my knowing what's more important about the conversation helps me have a better conversation. Better conversations mean stronger relationships.

Electronic Conversations

For many people, technology has changed the nature of conversation. It has even changed some people's definition of a conversation. The term *conversation* used to mean a face-to-face or at least an over-the-phone, real-time exchange that two or more people experienced together at the same time. The dictionary definition of *conversation* is "a spoken exchange of thoughts, opinions, and feelings." But not everyone shares that definition. Now when people refer to *conversations*, they often mean what I think is more accurately called an "exchange"—an exchange of information via email, text message, or IM.

There are times that technology threatens our ability to pay attention to people during conversations.

For example, a client reported that she had a one-on-one meeting with her supervisor once a week. But she feels more like it's a one-on-two meeting because her supervisor never comes to the meeting without her cell phone. The client feels like she's competing with her supervisor's phone for attention. If the phone buzzes with a text message or rings with a call, the supervisor answers. It doesn't matter what is happening in the face-to-face conversation; the electronic conversation wins.

Technology used to be something that brought people together. Families would gather around the radio, and later the television, to experience a program together. I remember huddling with my mom and my brother while we watched scary programs on television. But now, most households have multiple television sets, and several family members have some kind of tablet as well. So in most cases, even when the family members are watching something at the same time, they are not watching together. The family members are usually not all in the same room, and even if they are in the same room, they tend to be watching individual screens with earphones firmly blocking conversations with each other.

Phones are a particularly telling example of how we allow technology to stand in for real conversations. We text or email instead of calling. After all, it saves time and is more efficient. Right?

Sometimes an email is the most effective way to share information. Much of the time, report communication, which is primarily transactional, can happen effectively with email or text. Details about when and where a meeting will be held can be communicated by text. The percentage of increased sales over the last quarter can be communicated through email. Total costs of employee travel over the past two years can be shared with a team through email.

Other communication is best accomplished by a live, face-to-face conversation. Letting your child know what will happen if she keeps missing curfew needs a live conversation. Telling an employee he needs to improve his performance to keep his job needs a live conversation. Asking a neighbor to help you come to terms with your mother's illness needs a live conversation. This kind of conversation deserves more than a quick text. The people and relationships deserve more. Technology can get in the way. Choosing how to share information based on which is most effective (rather than which is easiest at the moment) increases your chance of success.

Choosing technology instead of a face-to-face conversation, moreover, can have serious consequences. A doctor explained to me the value of looking directly at a patient while she takes the medical history and discusses what to do next. She explained that unless she can look the patient in the eye and see that the patient understands, she doesn't feel he or she is ready to take the next step. Another doctor described this as seeing "the patient behind the pain." In other words, in addition to the symptoms themselves, it's important for the doctor to understand how the patient is experiencing the symptoms. The doctor can truly understand the patient's experience only through a deep conversation with the patient.

The current trend, however, is to value symptoms and technological record keeping more than conversations with patients. Instead of taking notes on paper during a conversation, the doctor now turns away from a patient and toward a screen to record the patient's information right into the computer. "So the patient is looking at the side of my face, not into my eyes," one doctor commented with dismay. This same doctor expressed concerns about his residents and their unwillingness to spend time with patients. He observed that the residents were more interested in quickly moving to diagnosis and action—possibly without a full understanding of the problem.

Spending time listening to patients is seen by some medical professionals as less important than treating them. But treating patients effectively takes a full understanding of the patients' symptoms and experiences. Entering symptom data into a computer doesn't provide this picture—in fact, focusing on the data can get in the way of the most effective treatment. Understanding how to treat a patient requires understanding the patient, and that takes a real conversation. The doctor who worried about patients talking to the side of his face shared this story. One patient complained of ongoing pain after an operation. The x-rays and other tests didn't indicate anything was wrong. When the doctor turned away from the computer to look at the patient, he asked different questions and gained new information. By really speaking with the patient, he discovered what was wrong. Only then was he able to treat her pain effectively.

Building Blocks of Personal and Professional Connections

Having Conversations That Build Relationships

Strong, healthy relationships help us live strong, healthy lives. That can help us avoid disease, cope more effectively with stress and problems, be more successful at work, and enjoy our lives more. There's no question that a strong social network can provide many significant benefits in all areas of our lives.

How do we develop these relationships?

One of the most effective ways to build, strengthen, and heal relationships—the kinds of relationships that bring enjoyment, lead to health and success, and sustain us in times of trouble—is through great conversations.[16] Communication experts such as Susan Scott and Deborah Tannen point to conversations as one of the best tools we can use to build relationships.

Just as conversations can build and strengthen a relationship, however, conversations can damage a relationship. A client of mine had a falling out with a family member that started with one bad conversation. The family member made an accusation, and my client just couldn't forgive him. Even a perceived slight can cause havoc. A colleague of mine belongs to a service group. Another member of that service group had misunderstood comments that were made in a casual conversation and called a formal meeting to complain. It turned out that the problem was imagined, but the hurt feelings and lack of trust that resulted were very real.

Any conversation can be the one that changes a relationship.

The good news is that we can build the kinds of relationships we want in our lives by having the right kinds of conversations. We can have real conversations that help build relationships and make things better.

Real conversations include the following elements:

- *A goal.* Real conversations have a clear goal, and that goal determines how the conversation progresses. What gets into the conversation and what gets left out of it, points that are covered and points that are not, questions that are asked, responses that are acceptable—all these are based on the goal.
- *Complexities.* People's motives and wishes—everything about us—can be complicated. Building relationships is complicated. Real conversations include complexities; they don't try to fit everything into predictable, small points. Complexities are messy and confusing, but real conversations include them anyway.
- *Cost.* There is a cost in having a real conversation. The cost of a real conversation includes being vulnerable, getting out of your comfort zone, and taking a chance you won't

be understood. But there is a greater cost in having a false conversation. Not having an honest conversation can result in a loss of trust, missed opportunities for growth, and possibly serious and lasting damage to a relationship.

- *Other people's needs.* Real conversations include the needs and goals and interests of other people. Real conversations recognize that if something matters to someone else, then that something deserves a conversation.
- *Silence.* Real conversations include time for thinking. That time for thinking usually happens in a conversation when people are not talking. Real conversations include times of silence.

Understanding comes from honest conversations. Honest conversations have a significant impact on relationships. These are the conversations that can be turning points. They matter. Honest conversations make thoughts and ideas real. We talk things into reality. You can change your relationships, your world, and your life one conversation at a time.

Conversations sometimes happen in your imagination, but the results show up in your life. If your head is full of negative, confrontational, competitive, or angry imagined conversations, these thoughts, feelings, and words will show up in your actual conversations. Having positive conversations with yourself can help you have positive conversations with others.

Building Work Relationships through Conversations

We build relationships in the workplace through conversations. Watercooler conversations and other informal conversations, as well as formal meetings, offer employees the chance to talk to each other. Some workplaces design space to encourage conversations among workers, recognizing the benefits of having a socially connected workforce.

Technology, however, tempts employees to choose efficiency over connection. When efficiency is the top goal in the workplace, it's easier to send an email or text instead of taking the time to have a conversation. This approach can work well for report or transactional communication: sending a quick email or text to the team that the meeting will start half an hour later than originally planned does seem a more reasonable choice than trying to stop by twenty desks or call twenty people. But email might not always be the most effective way to communicate.

Being able to have productive conversations is a necessary skill for professional success. A client came to me because she realized part of her job as a manager now included teaching her employees how to have conversations. She had a great new employee with terrific references and a solid education. She asked the new employee to call a vendor to resolve a discrepancy over a recent charge. The new employee sent an email, but it didn't resolve the problem. Problem resolution took a phone conversation, and the employee didn't know how to have one.

Supervisors are able to set the example of having face-to-face conversations instead of defaulting to email. One manager told me that when he joined a new organization, he started getting emails from his new employees. At the next staff meeting, he told his staff, "Don't email me. Come talk with me." The manager emphasized to me that he had been clear about speaking *with* him—he wanted to set the standard that he was looking for a back-and-forth conversation. He had to do some reminding, but before long, this manager was having conversations instead of reading emails.

Lack of conversation can lead to frustration and discord, as shown in Janet's story.

Case Study: Janet's Story

Janet had been working on a project for months, and she felt like things were going really well. Out of the blue, her supervisor

14

shifted her to another project. He didn't talk to her about it. He just announced it at a meeting. Janet was really angry and frustrated. She wanted to talk to her supervisor about it immediately, but she knew she shouldn't do it when she was upset. Instead, Janet asked if they could talk later. She gave herself a few days to calm down, and she practiced what she wanted to say. At the meeting, Janet was careful to be calm and specific about what she was upset about and why. Her supervisor admitted that he hadn't handled things well and apologized. Janet felt like they both developed more respect for each other in that conversation.

Janet was able to have a conversation with her supervisor because having open and honest communication was the norm around the office. Her supervisor encouraged his team to talk with him when they needed to. The abrupt assignment change was unusual and made Janet uncomfortable. That's why she decided to talk to her supervisor about it. The workplace might be primarily about work, but it's the relationships that make people and organizations successful. Because she could speak openly and have an honest conversation with her supervisor, Janet felt their relationship was stronger after an event that could have made it difficult for her and her supervisor to continue working together.

Building Personal Relationships through Conversations

Personal relationships, perhaps even more than workplace relationships, depend on conversations. Without the environment of work as something to share, personal relationships are vulnerable to emotions and misunderstandings.

People become friends because they discover shared interests, shared ideas, and shared feelings about politics or travel or the environment or other topics. Friendships grow or diminish in conjunction with the conversations that shape them.

When I moved into a new neighborhood, I first made friends with the people who were doing the same thing I was doing every morning: waiting for the school bus. As time went on, initial conversations revealed other things I shared with some of the parents, and I developed stronger relationships with them. I discovered that a couple of people were especially good matches for me. We started walking together to get some exercise after the bus left to take the children to school. Our conversations got deeper as we spent more time together, and we wanted to spend more time together as we discovered more about each other through our conversations.

Those friendships changed over the years, and so did the conversations. Based on the strong foundation of so many shared conversations, when we were in crisis over a child's decisions or a parent's failing health, we were able to share that experience with each other as well. I could reach out to them for help and know help would be there. Years have passed, and we continue to spend time together and share family triumphs and challenges. And all of that started so many years ago with simple conversations at the bus stop.

A client shared with me a similar evolution of a personal relationship. She became friends with someone she volunteered with. They began chatting while working together. Those conversations led to my client spending more time with this woman, and a strong friendship developed between them. When my client experienced a sudden tragedy in her family, it felt natural and safe to call her friend for help. The very serious conversation that these two people had was possible because of all the fun conversations they had shared over the years.

Even a brief conversation with friends can be a lifeline during times of stress.

Case Study: Anne's Story

A few years ago, Anne's husband was recovering from serious surgery. She was working extra hours to help pay the bills, and she was really tired. Her baby was especially cranky one night, and Anne just didn't think she could take any more. When the phone rang, the last thing she wanted to do was talk to anyone. But Anne answered anyway. It was a couple of teenagers from her youth group. Anne figured they needed a ride somewhere. She always wanted to help, but she didn't think she could manage to do one more thing that night. It turned out that the teens weren't calling to ask for a favor. They were calling to see if Anne needed anything. It meant so much. Years later, Anne can still remember how that made her feel.

A short conversation expressing concern reminded Anne of a relationship with two people who cared about her. This made her feel less alone. Years later, that feeling remains with her.

We build our personal relationships through conversations, including our conversations with family members. Being members of a family doesn't guarantee a healthy relationship. A healthy relationship is built through conversations in which we learn about people's interests, demonstrate support of people's goals, and accept differences in people's life plans. Children learn to trust their parents over time, based on a history of their parents being there and being willing to listen to them. Parents learn to trust children who are honest with them and share the good and the bad. Grandparents develop special relationships with a new generation— with grandchildren they sometimes don't understand—when they are able to have a series of conversations.

Family members who don't have conversations—face-to-face and phone conversations—lose an opportunity to develop this kind of relationship.

Conversations over the years about small, ordinary things might not seem to matter all that much, but what we learn through those conversations, including the things that make people smile and lean forward or frown and look away, contributes to building a strong and lasting relationship.

The Success That Matters Most

The Power of Conversations

Conversations can affect us more than we realize. After a series of surgeries and associated complications, I had to take a lengthy sabbatical from work. Since the surgeries were on my feet, I literally wasn't able to go anywhere. I withdrew from most of my activities. I went from spending most days surrounded by people and conversations to spending most days in the company of two cats.

As time went on, my lack of conversation with others made me feel not just alone, but lonely. I missed talking to people throughout the day. I felt like a different person, nearly unrecognizable to myself. As I started getting better and was able to spend more time with people, I felt more like myself again. I needed those conversations and those relationships in order to feel like myself.

From our personal lives to our social lives and work lives, conversations shape our relationships. Conversations can create, strengthen, and heal relationships. Even the shortest and smallest conversations can grow into something that lasts a lifetime. Think about what can come out of small talk.

We call it small talk, but this kind of talk doesn't need to stay small. It might start out that way. Many things start small and end up being really important. When you meet a new neighbor while you are both waiting for the school bus to come and pick up the kids, you engage in small talk. You say, "Where are you from?" to the new parent and ask the new child, "What grade are you in?" All of that might feel pretty small and unimportant. In reality, this is the way you demonstrate that you are listening and that you care. The next day or the next week, you remember where the new parent is from and mention something you saw on the news about that area. Now the small talk has a chance to grow.

If you show you care about the small stuff, then perhaps when the new neighbor has a medium-sized thing to say, she'll come to you. When she wants to talk about her new job and how nervous she is about her first presentation to the board, she'll mention it to you. You can have a conversation with her about it. And now your conversation isn't small anymore. It's growing, and it's becoming something that matters. Your conversations with this neighbor are helping you build a relationship.

Eventually, the neighbor's mother gets sick, and she really needs someone to talk to. This is a big deal, and she really needs a friend. She needs a relationship with someone who can help her through a difficult time. She can come to you about it because she has shared several small conversations and a bunch of medium conversations with you. Now she is able to come to you with something big. The conversations grew, and the relationship grew.

The right conversation can change everything.

We can improve our relationships with others by leaps and bounds if we become encouragers instead of critics.
—Joyce Meyer

CHAPTER 2

CHOOSING THE BEST CONVERSATIONS TO HAVE

> The real art of conversation is not only to say the
> right thing at the right place but to leave unsaid
> the wrong thing at the tempting moment.
> —Dorothy Nevill

The Power of Choice

Why Have a Live Conversation?

With an email or a text message, you are in control. No mess, no fuss. Write something down. Go get a drink. Come back and read it. Think about it for a few minutes. Make sure you use words that make you look good. Make necessary changes. Review it again. If you do all that, pause and review before hitting send, you can keep some distance from your emotions. You can stay in control.

Live conversations can quickly get messy. Messy, messy, messy. It might be hard to think up the right thing to say, and you might end up blurting out the wrong thing or something that makes you look dumb. You share yourself and your ideas in real time. Once you say something, you can't erase it. You can try to explain or even apologize and take it back, but once it's out there, it's out there. Conversations that happen live, in real time, don't give you the chance to go get a drink and think and find words that make you look good before hitting send.

So why bother with a live conversation? Because conversations are the real-time way we make real-life connections. Yes, you sometimes say the wrong thing. You ask a question that you shouldn't. You tell someone how you really feel or admit you don't know something, and the minute those words are out of your mouth, you regret having said them. Someone says something to you, and it makes you feel bad, and you wish you hadn't heard it. But you did hear it. You can't close your computer or put down your phone and walk away. You are still in front of that person with your hurt feelings, and you don't have privacy and space to figure out the perfect thing to say. You need to come up with something to say while you're still feeling all hurt and confused by the comment. There's no hiding. And if you say something horrible in return because you feel so awful that you can't think of anything else, you see the look on that person's face and know you made things worse. Once again, there's no place to hide.

And that's the moment when you figure out things about yourself and the other person and whatever it is that you're talking about. It's a messy process, and you say things you shouldn't say and hear things you don't want to hear. You keep trying to understand. You keep talking. You especially keep listening. You discover together. You learn things that you wouldn't have learned in a carefully edited exchange of text messages or emails. You discover ideas together that you never would have imagined on your own. You share things that are true. They come out in a conversation when you are feeling and listening and exploring and speaking all at the same time. You become so involved in the learning and exploring that you don't fix up your words to make yourself look good; you just keep going. And you say and hear truths you would never say or hear in the careful, edited, prepared-for-public-consumption world of text messages and emails.

So you choose to have a conversation even when it's hard. Sometimes conversations *are* hard. A friend of mine needs to have a conversation with his mother about his concern that it's not safe for her to drive anymore. This is not something she wants to hear, and it's not something he wants to say. He wishes it were safe for her to drive. He wishes that he could just pretend she could drive safely and that he could make excuses for the stop sign she didn't see or the curb she drove over the last time they went driving together. And he certainly wishes she would just decide she doesn't want to drive anymore. But the truth is, he must choose to have this conversation.

We all must choose to have important conversations, even when they are difficult.

A client wants to talk to her boss about a raise. She's been at this job for about a year. She has progressed quickly, meeting all the initial milestones that were set when she started the job. Because her work is so good, she's been asked to help out on a new big project. In addition, five months ago, her coworker left, and she took on the extra work caused by her coworker's absence. So by now, her workload doesn't look like her original job description. Her responsibilities have increased, but her salary has not. She wants to ask for a salary that matches the work she's doing now.

But it's so hard. It's hard to ask for more money. She wishes the management team would just recognize everything she's doing and realize she deserves a raise. They should. In an ideal world, they would. In the real world, they don't. So she needs to choose to have this conversation.

To Have or Not to Have

Should you always choose to have a conversation? No.

When you are just mad and just want to be mad out loud, choose not to have that conversation.

When you are hurt and want to hurt back, choose not to have that conversation.

When someone challenges you and demands that you answer right now and you know you cannot be productive or helpful on demand, choose not to have that conversation—at least, not at this moment.

When the conversation will make things worse for any reason, choose not to have that conversation.

When emotions are so high you can't have a conversation without those emotions taking over, choose not to have this conversation.

How do you choose when to have a conversation and when *not* to have a conversation?

Keep these questions keep in mind:

- Is this conversation likely to move us forward?
- Is this conversation necessary for the well-being of someone involved? (Even if it's tough, you must talk to your mother if you're worried about her driving; you must talk to a friend if you are worried about his drinking.)
- Is this conversation an important step for my personal or professional development? (Ask for the raise you deserve. Ask to be considered for a leadership position in your community. Don't wait for someone else to start the conversation; start the conversation yourself.)
- Is this conversation a reaction to an emotion and without any other purpose? (If you are so angry you can hardly speak, then it's best not to start this conversation.)

- Is this conversation an opportunity for me to learn something?
- Is this conversation an opportunity for me to strengthen a relationship?

Choose to have the conversations that promote understanding, strengthen relationships, and create goodwill.

Perspective

Sometimes an honest conversation can help you see things more clearly. For example, consider Carol's story.

Case Story: Carol's Story

Carol was stuck. She was unhappy in her work. She had a nagging health problem, and she couldn't figure out what to do about it. She felt like her life was on hold. One day she told a friend exactly how she felt. She was more honest than she had been in months—with herself and with her friend. Her friend listened carefully, heard what Carol was saying, and understood her frustration and fears. Her friend made a couple of suggestions that were what Carol needed to hear instead of what she wanted to hear. For Carol, that conversation changed everything. She left her job so she could find work that was fulfilling. She addressed her nagging health problem by changing her behavior and switching doctors. She took responsibility for her life. That one conversation gave Carol the courage to change.

This conversation was a game changer for Carol. She benefitted from her friend's honesty and concern. Carol and her friend had a strong relationship, and this conversation made it even stronger. It gave Carol perspective, direction, and the courage to change.

Choose What You Want the Conversation to Accomplish

Why are you having the conversation? What do you want to accomplish?

I often ask my clients to complete this sentence: "At the end of this conversation, I want …" In other words, what do you want to be different after the conversation?

Sometimes our emotions get involved, and we jump into a situation without thinking about where we want things in that situation to end up. That decision often gets us into trouble. I once got a call from someone who worked in another division. Our division had one shared project. The person who called me had seen a draft calendar I had put together months before, and based on that, she sent her team to a meeting on the wrong date. The calendar had been overhauled completely since my draft, and the updated version had been delivered to everyone (including the person who called me). But she had my draft calendar, and she decided the problem was my fault. After shouting at me about all the trouble I had created, she hung up on me.

I couldn't believe it. I had never been hung up on before—and certainly not at work. I mentioned this to a couple of coworkers sitting nearby. Both laughed, and one said, "Yeah, she's known for flying off the handle like that." They thought it was no big deal, but I was furious. So I called her right back, and I told her that it was not appropriate to hang up on me. And then—well, that's all I had. My entire reason for starting that conversation was to tell her I thought it was inappropriate to hang up on me. That might have been perfectly true, but it was certainly not reason enough to have a conversation—especially while she and I were both still so angry. Had I taken a moment to ask myself what I wanted to be different after the conversation, I would have realized I didn't have a good reason for having the conversation, and I would have resisted the temptation to make that call.

Here are some possible ways to complete "After this conversation, I want …"

- "I want my mom to understand that I love her and I'm worried about her safety when she drives."
- "I want my son to agree to do his homework when he gets home and not put it off until he's too tired to finish."
- "I want my boss to take me seriously when I make a suggestion."
- "I want my mom to let me take out the car after dark."

All of those are good reasons to have a conversation. The clearer you are about why you want to have a conversation, the more likely you are to be successful.

But you need to be honest with yourself. What do you *really* want? A client once told me, "I want to understand what would make this employee more successful" when she was preparing for a conversation with an employee. But the more I spoke with the supervisor to help her make a plan for this conversation, the more I realized that her real goal was for the employee to move on to another job. She didn't want to fire the employee, but she wanted the employee to leave. She wasn't being honest with herself about what she wanted, so she was preparing for the wrong conversation.

So, what do you really want to happen?

When you are clear about what you want to happen, take the time to consider how the result you desire will affect the other person. You want your mom to understand that it's not safe for her to drive and to willingly stop driving. But what will this mean for her? She won't be able to go to the grocery store on her own. She won't be able to visit her friends. She won't be able to visit you when she wants to. She will lose a sense of independence and control over her life. All of this matters to her—so it should matter to you. If you want to be successful in your conversation, you need to think about her.

The same line of reasoning applies to your son and his homework. You want him to do his homework without arguing or delaying or making up excuses. You want this because you don't want to spend every evening worrying about the homework and reminding him to do it and carrying that burden yourself. But what will it mean to your son? He will own responsibility for his homework. You won't keep reminding him. He can come to you for help, but other than that, he doesn't need to talk to you about homework. So there are definite benefits for him. You, on the other hand, will need to give up control. All of this matters to you both.

And when you want your boss to give you a raise, think about what it means to her. If you are making more money, it affects her budget. It increases her expenses. She might need to explain that to her supervisor. A raise for you might affect the rest of the team. Does everyone get a raise? What about other people at your same level throughout the organization? Your focus is on yourself and on the reasons you believe you deserve a raise, but you also need to consider how this affects your supervisor and your coworkers.

When you know where you want to end up—and how that goal affects the other people involved in the conversation—you can make a good plan for how to get there. You are more likely to be successful that way.

Choose Your Perspective

You can choose what you will believe about any conversation. We see actions and behavior. We hear words. We don't see and hear the intentions of the other person, the reasons that propel those words and actions. So, to help ourselves be able to understand the world around us and feel more comfortable, we tend to create a perspective from which to operate.

As long as we recognize that we choose our perspective, we can benefit by choosing a positive one. Here's an example of how that worked with me. I have worked with a woman for many years on a variety of projects. A few years ago, I went through some personal problems. I had to step back on some work projects, and I needed my colleague to take over some of my work. She did a few things, but she seemed to do them reluctantly. It was like she just left me there alone. At least that's how it seemed to me. I felt let down and disappointed. After all, if she wouldn't help me when I was in trouble, then why should I even keep working with her?

And then, thanks to some very helpful advice, I considered another perspective. What if she was trying to help and just didn't know what to do? Perhaps she was doing the things that would have been most helpful to her. I'd been assuming she didn't care about me, but maybe she was doing her best to help me in the best way she was able. What if I chose to believe she was doing her best and appreciated what she was doing instead of just resenting what she was not doing?

When I chose that perspective, I realized that I had never actually told her what I really needed. I thought that, after all our years together, she would just know. But this was a new situation for both of us, and sometimes even I didn't know what I needed. Once I started being more specific and clear—instead of expecting her to figure out on her own what assistance I needed—she was more able to help me. The more positive I chose to be, the more positive the situation became. The more I appreciated what she was doing, the more we understood each other. Operating from a positive perspective will help you choose positive words, examples, and gestures during your conversation. This will help you continue to move in the right direction.

We can choose our perspective; we can choose what to believe about ourselves and about others. And we can choose to believe as many positives as possible. If you become aware of your assumptions, then you can create the context that is most likely to lead to a successful outcome. Your perspective, what you choose to believe, will significantly influence your words and behaviors in your conversations.

Start by carefully choosing a perspective about yourself:

- You can learn something new and important. You do not know everything, but you have the capacity to learn. Other people can teach you.
- You can come to understand what other people believe and what they want. Understanding other people helps you have better conversations with them.
- You can build relationships with other people.

You can choose a perspective that serves your purpose for your conversation and then carefully and thoughtfully choose a perspective about the other person:

- Choose to believe that the other person in your conversation has positive goals for the relationship—even if they are not the same goals as yours.
- Choose to believe that the other person in your conversation deserves respect even when you do not agree; operating from a position of mutual respect is a significant contributor to success.
- Choose to remain positive, even if the other person does not; remember that if someone invites you to participate in a negative conversation, you can decline.
- Choose to commit to a successful conversation.

Choosing to make a commitment to the success of the conversation and choosing to operate from a positive perspective will help you make positive choices throughout the conversation.

Direction and Alternate Routes

Choose How to Control Your Response to What the Other Person Says

One way to recognize how much control you have over your conversations is to remember that you get to choose everything you say and every gesture you make. Every word. Every gesture. You choose every groan or "pffffft" or muttered "Oh brother." You choose every roll of your eyes or glance at your watch or scowl. You also choose every smile and encouraging "uh-huh" and indication of excitement and support. Most especially, you choose every response to what the other person says. No one makes you say something. You choose.

When you agree with what the other person is saying, or when you disagree and you think that what that person is saying is not important, it's not too difficult to keep control of your emotions and say something reasonable. But what do you do when your conversation partner says something completely ridiculous? I mean, *really* ridiculous. At that point, you can say whatever you want, right? Match ridiculous with ridiculous, right? Respond in kind. You can't really be expected to control yourself at that point, after all. Right?

Wrong. You *can* control yourself. You choose everything you say. You are responsible for everything you say.

Here are some tough but true things to remember about the choices you *can* make in conversations:

- You can and must control everything you say.
- You cannot control anything the other person says. You might influence it, and you can ask the other person to stop speaking in a way that is offensive or hurtful to you. But you cannot control whether or not the other person will change what she is saying or how she is saying it.

CAROL ANN LLOYD-STANGER

- You don't need to believe or agree with everything someone says to you. You can't stop someone from speaking, but you can choose not to accept what that person says.
- You can choose to have a positive conversation on your side by responding in positive ways to whatever the other person says.
- You can choose to leave a conversation that is not going in a positive direction.
- There are several ways to keep yourself on track if you are having a bit of a challenge keeping control of your responses.

Stephen Covey writes about the need to extend the time before stimulus and response. Someone else's words or actions are the stimulus. Someone challenges your suggestion. Or disagrees outright with your idea. Or ignores you. Or shouts at you. That's the stimulus. You'll want to respond immediately. Defend yourself. Defend your idea. Demand attention. Shout back. But that response doesn't help. To be in better control of your response, to choose a response that moves you toward your goal, you need space. Covey suggests you imagine pushing a pause button and take time to think about the wise, principle-based thing to do or say.[17] Resist the temptation to react. Stop and think.

Believe in your ability to control your words and actions. Remind yourself that you have the ability to maintain equilibrium even in the face of another person's storm. If you are invited to participate in a negative, name-calling, shouting, blaming, insult-trading conversation, *just say no*. You can do it. Never doubt your ability to maintain your self-control in a heated conversation.

Practice thinking before you speak. This is easier to do when you are not being challenged or shouted at, so practice during calm conversations. Tie your words to conscious thoughts in everyday conversations. Think about what you say and watch how others respond to your words and actions.

Try taking some practical steps toward controlling your words, tone, and actions in your conversations. When you feel yourself becoming upset, speak slowly and more quietly. When we're upset, we tend to speak more loudly and quickly. If you slow and quiet your speech, you'll begin to feel more in control. You can also change your physical position or take a drink of water or make some other kind of physical change. This can break your tension and be a physical reminder to you that you are in control of yourself.

Choosing your response and deliberately choosing your words and actions puts you in control of your conversation.

You can't control what another person says, but sometimes you can create an environment that takes the conversation in a more positive direction. Consider Emily's story.

Case Study: Emily's Story

Emily was in the middle of a performance review with her employee Janice. As usual, Janice was defensive about the areas where Emily felt improvement was needed. Although the company required that they have these reviews every six months, Emily felt they weren't doing much good. So she tried something else.

Instead of explaining what she felt Janice needed to improve, Emily asked, "How do you feel things went with this project?"

Janice was surprised by this question. "Well, I guess it went okay," she responded.

"Just okay?" Emily asked.

"Things didn't go as well as I had hoped," Janice said.

"Can you tell me more?" Emily asked.

By asking for Janice's real input, Emily learned what was behind Janice's decisions. Emily changed her approach, and she changed the direction of the conversation. By doing so, Emily learned what Janice was thinking and what Janice needed to hear. Rather than telling Janice what to do, Emily helped Janice take responsibility for improving her work. Janice left the conversation feeling eager and able to improve.

Emily's goal was to have a more productive review. She knew Janice would be more likely to improve her performance if she stopped being defensive. Saying, "Don't be defensive" is unlikely to work. Instead, Emily asked different, open-ended questions and encouraged Janice to keep talking. Given the space, Janice was able to identify ways to improve her performance.

Outcomes and Destinations

When to Keep Going and When to Stop

The more difficult the conversation is, the more it helps to make a conscious choice about whether to continue the conversation or not.

Just because a conversation hits a rough patch doesn't necessarily mean it should end. For example, if two members of a team disagree about the best person to handle publicity, they shouldn't just stop talking. They should take steps to make sure the conversation is productive, and they should figure out how to get a positive outcome.

Some conversations should continue. But not all. Sometimes we fall into a conversation because we react to a challenge, and then we realize that we made a bad move. Sometimes what started out as a productive conversation takes a bad turn. Sometimes emotions start to take control, and there's a chance one of you will say something that will do real damage. Sometimes you genuinely run out of things to say. For any number of reasons, some conversations should stop. Check out Kristin's story.

Case Study: Kristin's Story

Kristin met with Paula, her committee cochair, to discuss the status of the volunteers. The group had some big events coming up, and Kristin wanted to make sure there were plenty of people to run the activities. As they discussed some of the people who hadn't been as active as they had hoped, Paula said they should tell volunteers to show up more or leave the group. Kristin felt like they needed everyone—even people who had limited time. Paula felt they needed greater commitment. Pretty soon, Paula and Kristin were focusing on their disagreement about volunteerism and what *commitment* meant, and they were beginning to question each other's value to the organization. The conversation was headed in the wrong direction. When Kristin realized they were going down the wrong path, she asked for a break.

Kristin was wise to pause in her conversation with Paula. That pause gave them a chance to work through their frustration and get back to the conversation when they were ready to move forward.

Conversations that start out going nowhere or that take a wrong turn can do more harm than good. If you feel that your conversation is headed in the wrong direction, or in no direction at all, you can decide to end it. A neighbor once shared with me that she and her husband had made a pact not to talk about religion. She continues to go to church, and he does not. They support each other's decision. A conversation that consists of her trying to convince him to go to church with her or him trying to convince her to stay home with him is not productive. The last time they had one of those conversations, they decided to stop it. It was a mutual decision, reached in a friendly way.

There are hurtful and inappropriate ways to end a conversation, such as slamming down the phone or slamming the door shut. Slamming of any kind is usually bad for a conversation. Shutting down the other person after you've expressed your opinion is not a fair way to end a conversation. Leaving questions unanswered and walking away is also unfair. And leaving things unresolved can lead to problems down the road.

So how do you effectively end a conversation?

- Be honest. Say you think the conversation is headed in the wrong direction.
- Suggest a break and a time to start again.
- Maintain a positive perspective. Ending a conversation can be a positive thing.

Come up with a new perspective if you decide to try again. Address the things that sent things in the wrong direction the first time. Don't keep having the same conversation and expecting a different outcome. Albert Einstein is credited with having said that the definition of insanity is to keep doing the same thing and expecting a different outcome. The same is true of conversations—it's conversational insanity to have the same conversation in the same way and expect a different outcome. Bringing new ideas when you try again can result in a better conversation.

Finally, there are times when you decide to end a conversation because the cost to the relationship isn't worth the struggle in it. My mother always told me that the secret to successful parenting was to choose your battles. Perhaps the secret to success in life overall is to choose your conversations. If continuing a conversation will threaten or damage a relationship that you wish to maintain or will delay a necessary outcome in life or at work, the best decision might be to end that conversation. If you make this choice, be honest with yourself. End it. Let it go. Don't let it keep simmering inside you. If you want to revisit the topic of your conversation later, then say so, and say it clearly. If you say it's over, then mean it.

Choose which conversations should continue and which should end. Know why you make that choice—and take responsibility for making it work.

Choose Honesty and Respect

Honesty is necessary for a successful conversation. A lack of honesty can stop a conversation in its tracks. If you feel the other person is hiding something, your suspicion changes the conversation. You are more likely to become defensive or even evasive. If someone has betrayed your trust in the past, it's very difficult to be completely open with that person the next time. When your child was the only one in the house and says she doesn't know who could possibly have broken the vase she has been told not to play with, you have two issues to address: the broken vase and the lie. Children panic and try to avoid consequences, so they sometimes choose to lie. Unfortunately, adults do the same thing—and the consequences last much longer than being upset over a broken vase.

With conversations, always start by being honest with yourself. What do you want to be different at the end of the conversation? What do you *really* want? If something dark is lurking behind your public goal, you need to face it. Be honest with yourself about it.

Be honest about what you want and what you are willing to do to make it happen. If you want a program to change or you want to take your team in a new direction, then you need to make this clear. One of my clients was very disappointed when a member of the board of a small nonprofit resigned. My client had worked with this woman for nearly a year, and the resignation took her completely by surprise. It turned out that the woman had disagreed with the board about a new program for months, but she had never expressed her concern. "I feel like if I had known, we could have done something to figure it out," my client explained to me. "Instead, she said nothing for months and just left. I don't even know what her concerns were. It would have really helped if she had just told me."

But honesty doesn't mean that we forget about kindness. Let's pretend I just cut my hair short. I ask you, my good friend, "How does it look?" and I think I mean it. But perhaps I am looking not so much for total honesty as I am for a type of honesty that includes the fact that the haircut has happened and I can't undo it. So what I really want from you is a lot of kindness and a little reality. Don't tell me how much better I looked with long hair. That can't help me right now. Give me something I can work with. Give me feedback that helps. Suggest I try styling it with the part on the other side. Suggest highlights. Celebrate the idea of trying something new. Then take me to lunch.

The real value of honesty is that it respects the person and the situation. In the case of my client, hearing the truth from a board member during the discussion process would have been helpful. In the case of my imaginary haircut, hearing the truth that you hate my new hair would not have been helpful.

There's a scene in the movie *Apollo 13* where one more problem might endanger the crew on their reentry into the earth's atmosphere. One of the scientists points out the problem and asks, "Do you want to tell them?"

Gene Kranz, NASA flight director, asks, "Is there anything we can do about it?"

The response is "Not now."

Kranz responds, "Then they don't need to know, do they?" [18]

It's the truth, but knowing that truth won't help. The reality is that, in this situation, everyone has done the very best possible work to bring the astronauts home safely, and some truths don't help. The astronauts don't need to know about the latest problem because knowing about it won't help them solve it.

Tell the truth. Be honest. Participate actively in discussions and share your ideas and concerns. Take responsibility for your mistakes and get started fixing them. Give honest feedback. At the same time, always remember to show respect for the people involved. When it's no longer helpful to tell them something, leave that unsaid. Be focused on what will help. Be honest with yourself and others about what will help. Do everything you can to help. And always speak with respect.

Choose Next Steps

You continue to make choices throughout a conversation, right up to the end. However the conversation ends—because you have reached an agreement, said what you needed to say, or called for a break because things were going in the wrong direction—it needs to be clear what comes next.

After a tough conversation, it's tempting to just walk away and be glad it's over. The conversation went on as long as it was productive, and when it was over, everyone in the conversation was just happy to be finished with it. Perhaps you muttered, "Okay, thanks," "Sorry about what I said before," or something similar to those statements. But that's not enough.

Just as really great conversations can change everything for the better, really tough conversations can change everything for the worse. Tough conversations can weaken relationships. And in either case, whether the relationship was strengthened or weakened by the conversation, what happens next can make that change last.

After a great conversation, if there's no follow-up, it's difficult for the positive change to last. For example, my friend's son wants to change jobs. He met someone who could have been a great resource. They had a good conversation, and the potential resource encouraged the young man to follow up. But life intervened, one thing led to another, and the young man didn't quite get around to following up on that conversation. So any potential opportunities were lost. The conversation could have made a big difference, but not without follow-up.

Tough conversations that damage relationships also need follow-up. Unfortunately, when we don't follow up, the damage can become long lasting or worse than ever. A client described a situation that had this potential. She had an employee who made a series of mistakes, and in one case, my client really let this guy have it. She reprimanded him in front of coworkers. She knew it wasn't the right thing to do, but she was so frustrated, she did it anyway. Afterward, she had two choices. She was technically in the right since the employee had committed the same offense over and over despite being told to change his behavior. However, she didn't want to leave things on such a negative note. She arranged a follow-up conversation in which she apologized for the way she had delivered the news. She admitted that she had allowed her frustration to get the better of her, and she said she was very sorry to have gotten so angry in front of others. She did not retract her reprimand, but she did apologize for the delivery. The employee was happily surprised to have his supervisor do this. He accepted the apology and made a commitment to improve his behavior. The follow-up turned a potentially damaged relationship into a better one.

Not all conversations require follow-up. But some do. Here are a few general guidelines for choosing when and how to follow up on a conversation:

- Do you want something to change as a result of this conversation? Does the other person understand what you want to change? Are you sure? Does the other person agree? Are you sure? Do you agree on the time frame? Answers to these kinds of questions are often assumed rather than communicated. Be sure everyone agrees about what change should come from the conversation.
- Were questions left unanswered by the conversation? Some conversations leave things unsaid in order to cover the most time-pressing concerns. Leaving things unsaid can be a good conversational strategy, but lingering questions can slow or interrupt progress. Make sure everyone's questions

have been answered or arrange another opportunity to address them.

- Were feelings hurt? It's difficult to admit when we've had our feelings hurt at work, and it can also be hard to admit that in our personal relationships. If your feelings were hurt, you might avoid the other person in the future. If his feelings were hurt, the other person might avoid you. It might not be productive to rehash whatever caused the hurt feelings, but extra words of friendship or encouragement can help people feel better. Hurt feelings can make us withdraw from or work against another person, even when we don't realize that we are doing so. Making an effort to say positive things after a difficult conversation can help.

Choosing to follow up after a conversation allows you to have some control over its overall impact. The more positive you can be, the more likely it is that your conversation will lead to success.

We have control over our conversations. When we choose a positive perspective, say things that help, respect others, respond positively, and follow up, we are choosing to have conversations that build, strengthen, and heal relationships.

> The issues of the day have never seemed more complicated, and yet the conversations over how to solve them increasingly resemble cars passing down a divided highway. Whizzing by without a glance.
> —Lester Holt

CHAPTER 3

LISTENING AND UNDERSTANDING YOUR WAY TO SUCCESS

The greatest compliment that was ever paid me was when someone asked me what I thought, and attended to my answer.
—Henry David Thoreau

When people ask me about listening, they are usually asking how they can get other people to listen to them. Very few people ask me to help them develop better listening skills. However, learning to be a better listener is one of the most important things you can do to have better conversations.

Employers rank listening and communicating effectively as key factors in deciding whether an employee will be promoted. Most people appreciate someone who really listens. Being a good listener is a great step to developing personal and professional relationships.

Time to Learn

Listening Is the Part of the Conversation When We Learn

We recognize this in some ways. As children, we learn by listening to teachers and parents—even when we don't like it. As adults, when there's something we don't know anything about, we might listen to a webinar or podcast. But when we get into a conversation, we sometimes forget that we learn by listening.

Listening during a conversation is when you will learn what people are thinking and feeling about themselves, what people are thinking and feeling about you, and what people are thinking and feeling about the topic.

The more you listen and learn, the better prepared you'll be for the conversations that you have from then on. You will know what matters most to the other person, and that helps you understand how to craft your own message in order to promote understanding. You will learn opinions and ideas that might clarify your own thinking. You'll have a sense of where the other person is coming from, what the other person's priorities are, and how you might help that person learn from you as well.

It's usually easier to be effective in conversations when you are speaking with people you know. Get to know the other person better in your conversation by listening. Listening will help both of you be more effective. Consider Doug's story.

Case Study: Doug's Story

Doug assembles a great, hardworking team to work on a project. They are creative and really good to work with. The work is complex, and there are several problems that need to be addressed, so it's not surprising that there's confusion sometimes. Having confusion isn't necessarily a problem. But Ellen responds to being confused by talking. She talks about all the things that can go wrong, past projects, what she has already done, and what she is thinking about doing next. Her talking makes it hard for other people on the team to think clearly. Doug sometimes tells her to be quiet. Doug believes if Ellen would just listen instead of talking, she would understand the project—and everyone on the team would be able to solve problems more quickly.

Ellen's response to confusion or questions is to talk. That choice stops her listening and makes it nearly impossible for her to understand what she needs to do next.

A few steps can help us be more successful in listening:

- *Listening to and understanding others before you talk.* Conversations give us an opportunity to learn, and this happens when we listen. When we listen, with the intent of understanding, we can transform relationships. It's tempting to stop listening when we disagree with what's being said. Not agreeing with others is a reason to try harder to understand them. Understanding may help you find areas of agreement or at least increase your ability to deal with disagreement in positive ways. The more you understand others, the more effective you will be when you speak with them. Get them to tell you their stories.

- *Respecting others.* The dictionary definition of *respect* is to hold in esteem or honor. In practical terms, this means to have conversations where you listen, let others finish speaking without interruption, believe in their abilities, and recognize that their truths are valid to them. It helps to think about what you can learn from the other person. What is interesting about her perspective and opinion? Try to remember that the other person's "right answer" is as valid to her as yours is to you. In fact, there can be more than one right answer. When you value difference, you learn.

Respecting others as you listen can lead to hearing some
great new ideas.

- *Using language to its potential.* Language is one of the greatest
tools we can use to create, maintain, and strengthen our
relationships. The way we use language demonstrates our
commitment to listening. We create reality through our
language. Words matter. When you are thinking about
relationships, what words invite others to speak and help
a relationship grow stronger? Body language is another
important language. Smiling and looking at the other
person in friendly ways help reinforce your commitment
to listening. We share ideas through words and gestures.
Using language to its potential will support listening and
help build strong, lasting relationships.

What People Want

People talk because they want something. They don't always say
exactly what they want. They might not even know exactly what
they want. But remember that if someone is talking, that person
wants something.

I had a client learn this the hard way. She moved into a new
neighborhood, and immediately her neighbor stopped by and started
telling her about his garden. She wasn't interested in gardening, so
she didn't really listen. A few weeks later, the neighborhood held a
weekend picnic. My client was annoyed to find herself stuck in a
conversation with this same neighbor, who was once again going on
and on about his garden. After a few bored "Uh, um, uh-huh"-type
of comments, she managed to escape and meet someone new. Days
later, she came outside to find her neighbor in her yard cutting the
branches off her tree. She was stunned and shouted at him to stop.
Now *he* was stunned. He had asked about trimming the tree at

BUILDING RELATIONSHIPS ONE CONVERSATION AT A TIME

the picnic, and she had said, "Um, uh-huh." Of course, she had no memory of this. She hadn't heard him. She hadn't been listening.

This neighbor had been talking because he wanted something. He wanted a couple of things. He wanted to talk about his garden. But he also wanted more sunlight for that garden, and the way to get more sunlight was to have fewer branches on my client's tree. When he talked about trimming the tree, and he heard "uh-huh," he thought that was permission. But my client hadn't been listening. She didn't realize he wanted something. She thought her sounds were meaningless. They were meaningless to her. They were permission to him.

Most picnic conversations don't lead to someone cutting branches off a tree, but we do get into trouble when we forget that people talk because they want something.

Here are some tips to help you figure out in a conversation what someone wants:

- Remember that if someone is talking, there's a reason why. There's a good chance that the person wants something. Listen.
- If you can't figure out what the person wants, ask. You don't need to be confrontational. "What do you want?" can easily sound confrontational. Try saying, "Is there something you would like me to do about this?"
- Be patient if the person isn't sure what he or she wants. Some people need some time to figure out what they want and need. See if you can help. Maybe try saying something like "I understand if you're not sure what you need right now. I have a meeting, but I'd be happy to talk later."

People talk for all kinds of reasons. They aren't always plotting to get something out of you. But they want something. Perhaps they want to make a personal connection. Perhaps they long for human contact. They might want to try out a new joke or a story. Good friends want to share important events in their lives. Coworkers want to let you know the status of a project.

Sometimes people talk without such a clear purpose. They start just talking about a garden, and they slip in something about cutting branches off your tree. There is no way to eliminate all possible misunderstandings. But if you remember that people who are talking usually want something and if you listen to them carefully, you will have a better chance of figuring out what they want. Understanding what people want can lead to great discoveries. This happens in Sheri's story.

Case Study: Sheri's Story

Sheri was driving her niece Diane to the museum so Diane could complete a school project. Sheri noticed her niece commenting on other cars, the weather, and what was on television the night before. It seemed to Sheri that Diane might be trying to say something else. So she asked how Diane felt about the project at the museum. That got Diane talking. As it turned out, Diane was really worried about the project and about the class in general. She wasn't sure what the teacher wanted. That made her think she might not get a good enough grade to get into college. Diane was looking for some reassurance. So she started talking. She had just been waiting for someone to listen.

By demonstrating her willingness to listen, Sheri encouraged Diane to talk. The more Sheri listened, the more she learned. Sheri was able to help Diane because she first listened to her.

To Build a Bridge

People usually share what they are thinking more easily than what they are feeling, but what they are feeling sometimes has a greater impact on what they say and do. The more we listen, the more we'll understand about the thoughts and feelings of others.

The simple act of listening communicates your willingness to take someone seriously. That can be an important step in getting another person to be honest and open. If you make time to listen to your daughter, that action communicates your affection for her. Even if you can't answer all of her questions or solve all of her problems, the very act of listening is reassuring to her and strengthens your relationship. The trust that your daughter develops will make it easier for her to turn to you in the future. Listening works the same way with other people.

Listening builds trust. Taking time to listen to someone and really trying to understand her will make it easier for her to come to you next time. The more you listen, the stronger bond you will create between the two of you. When the difficult, heavy conversation comes, that connection between you and the other person will be strong enough to handle the more difficult parts of the conversation. When you listen, your relationship becomes stronger and more able to survive difficult conversations.

Listening validates others. Think about a conversation between a customer and a customer-service representative. The customer calls because something is wrong. If the customer-service representative becomes defensive or implies or states outright that the customer has done something wrong, the customer becomes even more upset. The best way that the customer-service representative can help the customer is by listening to the customer first and letting the customer explain what went wrong. Then, once the customer has had the chance to be heard, the customer will be more likely to listen to the way to solve the problem.

When people have something difficult to say, they often focus on how to get the message out. They might wonder about what words and gestures will have the best effect. They think about which details to include. They may rehearse their part of the conversation to make sure their delivery is just right. But they often forget an important step: to listen. You will be more successful delivering difficult news (or any other kind of news, for that matter) when you listen first. Hearing and understanding what matters to the other person will help you shape the news in the right words and in the best delivery style.

Listening demonstrates that you care. It shows that you are willing to take the other person seriously and give real consideration to other views and ideas. It gives you the opportunity to hear frustration and fear and to understand what really matters to this person. Listening helps you know what matters most and what will be most effective. Listening builds a bridge of understanding that will promote more effective and more productive conversations in the future.

There are different ways of listening effectively. Understanding these styles will help you be a better listener to all kinds of people, including people whose styles are different from your own. People can be grouped according to their listening styles:

- *Highly interactive listeners* talk alongside the other person, asking questions and making suggestions.
- *Participatory listeners* join in the conversation at times to agree with and support the person who is speaking.
- *Highly receptive listeners* mainly nod and smile, not speaking much.

Of course, these are not absolute categories, and not everyone falls firmly into one category or another. These categories are more of a continuum with highly interactive listeners on one end, highly receptive listeners on the other end, and participatory listeners in the middle. Everyone falls somewhere along the continuum.

A mismatch can be a problem. When someone prefers to be in a conversation with a receptive listener and is faced with someone chattering alongside him, he's not going to be comfortable. Likewise, if someone prefers a highly interactive listener and her conversation companion sits quietly and smiles, the speaker will feel a bit troubled because she perceives that her companion is not really listening. Meeting someone's expectations by matching your listening style to hers will reassure her that you are listening and care about what she is saying.

How do you match your listening style to the style of other people in conversations? First, you need to understand that different listening styles are differences, not deficiencies. There is no one *right* style. In fact, most of us don't even think about listening styles. But being aware of styles can help you be a better listener. Trying different styles can be helpful. If you tend to naturally fall on the receptive-listener end of the continuum, find a friend who is very chatty and try to talk alongside her. If you find it natural to participate alongside someone who is speaking, then seek out someone who is naturally quieter. Ask that person some questions, and practice more receptive listening, resisting the temptation to chime in if he slows down. It takes effort, but practicing styles that don't come naturally to you will help you be more effective.

Generally speaking, people have listening styles that reflect their speaking styles: those who find it easy to strike up a conversation and easily and happily carry the conversation tend to be very interactive listeners. And those who are reticent to start a conversation, those who hold back and are happy to make small contributions rather than running the conversation, are likely to be receptive listeners.

When you are just getting to know someone, try different styles and monitor the response. For example, you can begin somewhere in the participatory mode, carefully monitoring the other person's reaction to your listening. If the other person smiles when you participate, you can try to be a bit more interactive. If the other person seems startled when you start talking, you can pull back toward the receptive end. You'll learn what works best as you keep listening. In other words, the more you listen, the more you'll know how to listen most effectively.

Listening is the gift that just keeps on giving!

Questions That Get Answers

It's hard to be a good listener when no one is talking. To get people talking, ask really good questions.

Ask questions that make people feel smart and validated, not like they need to come up with the right answer. Ask people for their opinions. Encourage them to share their ideas and plans. Be interested in what they say. Remember that the more people talk, the more you can learn.

Invite people to respond to your opinions and ideas. Be curious about their answers. Resist the temptation to jump in and defend your ideas when people question you. Your ideas can't make a real impact in the world until they are out in the world. Invite other people to respond honestly to your ideas. Value their responses. You might not agree, but hearing others' responses will help you communicate your ideas more effectively.

Ask people to explore thoughts and other alternatives with you. As you speak and listen together, you might discover something that neither of you would have thought up alone. Discovering new ways of thinking can lead to powerful learning.

Asking questions can uncover new ways of thinking and new ideas. Sometimes people hesitate to ask questions because they are afraid of looking foolish or unprepared or stupid if they don't know the answers. You can learn the answers—but only when you admit you don't already know everything. Ask questions to learn what you don't know.

There are questions that tend to shut down people and bring an unfortunate end to conversations. Avoid these:

- Questions that invite justification: "Why did you make this decision?" or "How could you think this would work?"

- Questions that are thinly disguised accusations: "Whom do we have to thank for this latest problem?"
- Questions that have a right answer: "What is the most effective way of getting this report done?"

Instead, ask questions that help you and the other person make discoveries. Here are some ways to ask questions that will get a conversation going:

- Starting with phrases like "What do you think about ..." and "What do you think might help us do ..."
- Making it clear there are no right or wrong answers, for example, by asking, "Can you tell me more about ..."
- Asking for genuine feedback, such as by starting with "What do you think we do well?" and then moving to "What do you think we could do better?"
- Gathering ideas before making a decision, for example, by asking, "What do you suggest we consider here ..."
- Breaking complex problems into manageable steps, such as by asking, "What is one thing we could do to start things moving in the right direction?"
- If something didn't go well, emphasizing the opportunity to learn by asking, "What would we do differently if we could start over?"
- Demonstrating your desire to learn from others by asking questions such as "Is there anything I haven't asked that you'd like me to know?"

Asking questions can be a way to start learning. Ken's story is an example of how asking questions can lead to success.

Case Study: Ken's Story

Ken needed extra effort from his production team over the next month. There were six projects due in the next four weeks. Ken knew he would have to offer something to make all that extra work worthwhile. Ken had the authority to offer either overtime pay or time off (comp time). How did he decide which to offer? He asked. Ken asked each person on the production team. Ken thought everyone would choose the money, but he learned that about half of his team wanted the time off. Asking the question gave Ken the information he needed to be successful.

Ken was prepared to meet his team's needs because he asked questions. By asking questions that uncover new information—not questions that seek to verify what you already think—you'll move forward in a conversation, in a relationship, or on a project. You'll become able to make better decisions.

Sometimes asking a risky but necessary question can really set things in motion. Judy's story is an example of how a thoughtful question can be a game changer.

Case Study: Judy's Story

Judy was hired by an organization to coach one of the managers. When she met the new client for the first time, he told her he thought the coaching was a complete waste of time. He said he was happy to sit in the room with her for the appointed time but that she should bring a book or something because he was not about to explore his feelings or brainstorm new ways of thinking and acting. He said he was good at his job and had his own way of doing things and his own way of working with people and that was just the way it was. Judy could have stormed out or defended her work or marched over to the manager and revealed the client's resistance. Instead, she asked the client a question: "How is that working for you?"

That question was tough to ask, and Judy had no idea how the man would respond. As it turned out, he took the question seriously and admitted that his way of working with people wasn't working all that well. The question was the turning point for that conversation, for the relationship between Judy and her client, and for the client's making changes necessary to create the professional—and personal—life that he wanted. Judy's question was the first step in her client's success.

Committing to Being a Better Listener

If you want to be a better listener, there are steps you can take. It might not be easy, but it will be worth your effort. You can improve your ability to listen in a conversation by taking these steps:

- Start by setting a specific goal of listening. Believe in the benefits.
- Prepare to listen. Be open-minded. You might not agree with what that person is saying. You might even be strongly opposed to what that person is saying. Listen anyway.
- Stop talking. This is easier for some people than for others. You can't really listen and talk at the same time. So stop talking. Give others space to talk.
- Pay attention. Don't tune out. Focus on this person. Concentrate. Keep your mind on the person and on what she is saying.
- Value the perspectives of other people. When you value other people's ideas, you'll find it easier to make the effort to listen.

- Encourage the other person to speak. Don't interrupt or jump in, even if the other person is talking about you. Just listen.
- Remember that purposeful listening can reduce conflict. People often need to be heard before they can calm down. Listening to someone can reduce feelings of frustration and the likelihood of acting out.
- Pay attention to tone, especially if it changes. It's easier to control the words we choose than to control our tone. In other words, someone's tone can give you a good sense of when that person is getting upset, even if he doesn't say so.
- Pay attention to body language. If someone avoids eye contact, she might be uncomfortable about something. If she folds her arms and closes herself off, there could be a reason. Pay attention to what the whole person is saying.

Listening can be difficult, and effective listening takes effort, patience, and dedication. The good news is that there are many benefits to good listening.

Listening makes you smarter. You gain knowledge, knowledge, and more knowledge. You gain understanding of other perspectives on an issue. With important or complex issues, this greater understanding is an important tool in your moving forward. You gain information that you can apply to other problems. These ideas might never have occurred to you if you hadn't been listening. You lower your chances of making a mistake because you better understand the other person and the situation.

The more you listen to other people, the more you will be appreciated. You will earn a reputation as a good listener and as a person who understands. People really appreciate being listened to. When you become a good listener, people will seek you out.

You can certainly ask to be heard, even by an unwilling listener, especially if you have demonstrated a willingness to listen yourself. If a person does not seem inclined to listen to you, you can remind him that you have made an effort to listen first. Of course, that won't guarantee that he will listen to you, but it increases the likelihood that he will. You made the effort to understand him. That's a good start.

We spend more than half of our working and social time communicating—some suggest as much as 70 percent.[19] Listening will make you better at all areas of communication. Your relationships will improve. You will be better at your job. You'll be a better parent. You'll be a better friend.

In fact, you can be more effective in all areas of your life if you keep working on being a great listener.

Demonstrating That You Are Listening

Your body shows you are listening. Friendly eye contact, leaning forward, an open posture, smiles, and nods say, "I'm listening." On the other hand, looking out the window or at the clock, or looking around the room for someone else to talk to says, "I'm not listening." Saying, "Go ahead—I'm listening" while you glance around the room, shuffle papers on your desk, or check your watch sends conflicting messages. People will believe your actions more than your words.

Perhaps the most difficult step to take these days is putting away your phone. When you are looking at your phone during a conversation, either you are listening to the conversation or you are checking email or Facebook on your phone. You are not doing both. If you need to finish an email before you can listen, just say so. Finish the email, and then turn your full attention to the person who is speaking. Listening takes concentration and focus. We have become a society that fools itself into thinking we can do anything and be on the phone at the same time. We think we can walk and check our phones. We think we can have dinner and check our phones. We think we can talk to friends and check our phones. We even think we can drive and check our phones. We can't. Attempting to do so is disruptive, rude, and dangerous. We need to put down our phones and listen to each other.

Put all your attention into what the other person is saying and not into planning your response. It's tempting to wait until the speaker pauses or takes a breath or just slows down a bit so you can jump in and take over the conversation. If you're planning your response, you are not listening to the other person. Concentrating on the other person will help you pay attention to what she is saying.

As you take listening more seriously, you will find yourself understanding other people. The more you understand, the better conversations you can have—and the stronger your relationships will be.

Listening Builds Relationships

These are some things to keep in mind about listening:

- The busier you are, the more you need to listen. Listening effectively prevents mistakes and promotes understanding.
- Don't hear someone else's words through your own opinions. If you set your opinions aside, you can encounter the ideas of others.
- Keep others talking. If you stop talking, you can encourage others to talk more.
- Actively participate in the successful exchange of ideas.

Listening is a key to successful relationships, both on a professional and on a personal level.

Ways Listening Can Strengthen Relationships

One of the most common complaints that human resource representatives hear is that employees feel like their managers don't listen to them. Feeling like their managers don't listen can make employees feel less invested in the success of the organization and less effective overall. Feeling like others are listening to them, on the other hand, can help these employees become more engaged at work.

Listening skills are rated highly by people in leadership positions: managers, community leaders, and parents. Managers often rank listening skills among the most important competencies needed for success. According to Nancy J. Foster, the director of the Northern California Mediation Center, listening is the foundation of good communication.[20]

Good listening saves time and money at work. In addition to feeling that others are listening to them, employees who listen—to each other, to managers, to customers—are more effective in doing their jobs. Listening to customers is particularly important in saving time and money in the workplace.

Listening effectively can be a powerful way of increasing the way you understand people and make you more able to respond to them in meaningful ways. Penelope found that out.

Case Study: Penelope's Story

Penelope had developed a good relationship with Tom, one of the contractors in the Seattle office. When Tom came to town on a business trip, Penelope was happy to meet him in person. They agreed to have dinner together after the meetings. At dinner, Penelope noticed that Tom seemed distracted and kept checking his phone. She asked if anything was wrong. Tom took a moment, and then he took a deep breath and said his mother had just been diagnosed with Alzheimer's. He was clearly shaken up about it, and Penelope wanted to help. She had just read a couple of articles about Alzheimer's and had seen something on television about it, so her immediate thought was to jump in and share all the encouraging information she had just learned. But Penelope remembered to listen first. So she asked if Tom wanted to talk about it, and then she kept quiet. Tom really opened up. It seemed to help him to have someone listen to him. He talked about his mother's case and what the family was especially concerned about. Penelope realized all the things she thought she knew had nothing to do with Tom's situation. Her talking wouldn't have helped him; her listening helped him tremendously.

When you listen, you understand things that help you be more effective in all areas of your life. Although Penelope's conversation was about a personal matter, it happened between coworkers. It strengthened their relationships, which will spill over into work. Stephen Covey said it this way: "Seek first to understand, then to be understood."[21] Listening can change everything.

> I like to listen. I have learned a great deal from
> listening carefully. Most people never listen.
> —Ernest Hemingway

CHAPTER 4

EXPLORING STYLE AND MAKING CONNECTIONS

I've long believed that if you understand how conversational
styles work, you can make adjustments in conversations
to get what you want in your relationships.
—Deborah Tannen

Sometimes people tell me their conversations aren't working—and they can't figure out why. They say things like this:

- "My supervisor never understands what I'm trying to say to him."
- "I say something that seems fine to me, but my neighbor gets really mad. I don't understand why."
- "I'm having trouble talking to a coworker. I keep trying harder, but it seems like the harder I try, the worse things get. It's not like there's some big disagreement. We just don't seem to be able to understand each other."

Image and Expressions

People choose to express themselves, to tell you a bit about their personalities and preferences, through something we often call style. One way to see this is through the way people dress. Our clothing is one way for us to take on a particular style. Characters in a television show or a movie communicate their personalities through their styles. The television series *Downton Abbey* progresses through different time periods, and the time periods are marked in part by the changing outfits people wear. We don't need to see images of newspapers with the year prominently displayed—we know times are moving forward as the outfits change.

In addition to the general shifts in time, different characters' clothing tells us a great deal about the way they respond to the world. The Dowager Countess changes very little in her clothing, which reflects her character's personality and general resistance to change. Lady Sybil shocks her family when her choice of a new dress pushes the boundaries of what's acceptable. Later, Lady Mary communicates that she is moving on from the death of her husband as her clothing becomes more fashionable. Eventually, she lets us know she is a modern woman when she cuts her hair in the latest style. Even Lady Edith steps out of the family home and into the modern world, and her clothing begins to reflect her changing character. Her outfits as she takes on this new role are appropriate for a working woman instead of a woman of leisure.[22]

The importance of clothing in period pieces is reflected in the term often used to talk about programs like this: costume dramas. But it's the differences in the characters' clothing that really tells us something about them. It's their style we are interested in—we meet that first through their clothing. And interest in style is not limited to televised dramas.

Think of what people in your office communicate through their styles. What impressions are they trying to create? What about people in your neighborhood? What do you think Steve Jobs meant to communicate through his signature outfit—jeans and a black shirt—whenever he introduced new products?

In addition to clothing, people communicate style through the cars they drive, the way they decorate their desks at work or in their homes, and even the food they eat. After all, you can usually count on a $40,000 car to start reliably each morning and get you to the office. Why are some people willing to pay $400,000 for a car instead of $40,000? The additional money doesn't buy ten times more reliability. It buys style.

I remember a conversation with my grandfather when I was a senior in high school. I was asking for help buying my first car. My grandfather kept saying, "You just need something that will safely and reliably get you from one place to another." I wanted more. Yes, I wanted something safe and reliable. But I also wanted something that looked young and snazzy. I wanted to choose the color. I wanted to have a car that made a statement about me. My grandfather actually understood that. He always drove a particular brand of car, not so much for its rating in *Consumer Reports* as for its look. Successful businessmen of his generation drove that brand of car. It was part of his image. It was part of his style.

Wearing autographed Air Jordans doesn't buy you a speedier run or more consistent layups. The Tiffany engagement ring doesn't guarantee that your marriage will be better. The popularity of those products is not about function. It's about style.

People also have conversational styles.

What is style? It's a way of expressing your preferences, your interests, your self-definition, your sense of your place in the world, or your aspirations. It's a way of telling people who you are. You wear certain clothes, drive a certain car, and decorate your office in a certain way. You also have conversations in a particular way. You communicate yourself through your style.

Understanding conversational style and being able to use the most effective style in each conversation will help you be more successful.

Why People Don't Get You

When conversations go wrong, it can be enormously frustrating. When we can't figure out why, it's even more frustrating. And when we try to fix what's wrong and somehow keep making things worse, it's enough to make us want to give up.

And then there are the things we want to be able to do but feel we can't. I've heard people say things like this:

- "I wish I could speak up in meetings like Karen does, but that's just not me. She's confident about things like that. I'm not."
- "Marie can always think of something to say—even when she's not prepared. She runs into the president of the company, and instead of getting nervous and tongue-tied, like I do, she is able to say something interesting and intelligent. I just stand there desperately trying to think of something to say that won't make me sound like an idiot. I never succeed."
- "Laurie always knows just what to say. If anyone has a problem, they head right to her. And they always feel better after talking to her. I wish I could be like that. She seems to be able to get along with everyone."

People are frustrated because they can't make conversations work, they can't figure out how to get people to understand them, they can't manage to speak up in stressful situations, and they don't know what to say to people. They want to, but they feel like they can't.

All these problems—people misunderstanding you, your conversations not working despite your best efforts to fix them, not being able to speak up in meetings, or struggling to think of something to say when you're put on the spot—have something in common. It's not about you. It's about style.

We all have a conversational style. It's the basic way we approach conversations: private conversations with family or friends, public conversations in meetings or in front of people. It's our delivery method, the way we share with others.

"It's Just the Way I Am"

One of the most challenging things about conversational style is that people don't usually recognize that they have one. Conversational style develops over time, often being influenced by someone's upbringing. So the way you learned to speak in your family or school environment, the way people talked to each other in your neighborhood and community, the ways you learned to negotiate with parents and teachers to get what you wanted—all this contributed to your conversational style. And you probably weren't even aware of it.

The people around you have had the same experience. Friends, neighbors, and colleagues develop their styles. The larger your community becomes, the more diverse it becomes—and the more conversational styles you encounter.

We can spot conversational styles if we listen carefully. Some people express themselves in direct ways, just asking for what they want. Others are less direct, preferring to chat for a while before making a request. Some people start conversations easily, greeting strangers and friends with equal pleasure. Others have a harder time making conversation and usually wait for others to get things started. These patterns evolve based on what works and feels comfortable. That means the way we have conversations seems natural to us, the *normal* way of communicating. Over time, we settle into a conversational style that is comfortable and generally useful. It doesn't take much effort to listen and speak and ask questions in this way. We simply express ideas and opinions. Tonya's story is an example of what can happen when styles don't match up.

Case Study: Tonya's Story

Tonya's team has been unhappy lately—the members feel like they're overlooked (and sometimes overrun) in department decisions. The all-staff lunches are a good example. Someone else always makes the decision about who's catering, with no recognition that some people on Tonya's team are vegetarians. Tonya decided to bring up the subject of staff lunches with the manager, Kendra. As soon as Tonya mentioned that some people were unhappy with the staff lunches, Kendra started asking questions. What didn't they like? Why not? Vegetarians? Who's a vegetarian? How many vegetarians are there? What would they like to eat? Tonya felt like she was being interrogated. It wasn't that there was anything wrong with the questions, but Kendra was so loud and so fast that Tonya couldn't even think. Tonya's answers were accurate, but the conversation felt incomplete to her. Kendra was finished, however, and said she would get some salads next time. Before she knew it, Tonya was out in the hall walking to her desk. She couldn't figure out why she felt so bad. Kendra offered to get salads, so she seemed to agree about adding vegetarian options to the staff lunches, but Tonya still somehow felt like she hadn't been heard.

Why does Tonya still feel misunderstood? The specific request—to have vegetarian options at the staff lunches—was addressed, but Tonya still feels like her manager doesn't listen. Kendra, the manager, thinks Tonya got what she wanted, but Tonya still feels bad. She wants to be understood. One problem was solved, but she doesn't feel like Kendra understood what was really wrong.

The real problem isn't the content. The problem is the style. Sometimes conversations break down because people have serious disagreements about important issues. But lots of conversations fall apart in the way that Tonya's did. Tonya and her manager agreed that the group needed different options for lunch. But even though she ended up with salads being added to the lunch selections, Tonya didn't feel like she'd really been heard. She still felt uncomfortable, as if she'd been pushed into something. In cases like this, the problem isn't the topic. It isn't the substance. It's style. Kendra, the manager, didn't realize that her abrupt style meant that her effort to fix the food problem hadn't really helped.

Style preferences tend to become more pronounced when we feel stressed. I like to compare this to our *style* of driving on the right (as in "not on the left," not as in "correct") side of the road in the United States. I spent some time in the United Kingdom in graduate school. People drive on the other side of the road over there. One of my friends from the United States bought a car while in the UK. He carefully reminded himself to drive on the left. But one night, it was raining, visibility was low, traffic was heavy, and someone pulled out in front of him. Without thinking, my friend reverted to his usual style of driving and pulled the car sharply to the right side of the road—right into oncoming traffic. Fortunately, the other driver was used to the rain and traffic and made adjustments. Everyone was fine.

Under stress, natural style takes an especially strong hold. And, just like when my friend pulled the car to the right without even thinking, we sometimes use a style without being aware that we are using it. We magnify natural tendencies. Tonya felt stressed when she was speaking to Kendra, so her naturally hesitant style became even more pronounced. She had wanted to talk about the way her team felt overlooked—not just about salads for lunch. The louder Kendra got, the more stressed Tonya felt, and the quieter she became.

But style can change. We can use a different style when our natural styles aren't working.

There are a variety of quizzes and assessments available to test your communication style. But fitting yourself firmly into a single category implies a sense of permanence that can work against you. Being able to recognize style as changeable and being able to adapt your style are easier if you recognize that style is more like a sliding place along a continuum than a fixed point in a box.

Imagine a conversation-style continuum with most of us falling somewhere between these extremes:

Direct Doris
Always gets right to the point without any small talk or rapport talk; tends to offend people

Indirect Isabelle
Has trouble saying exactly what she wants and needs; tends to confuse people who can't figure out what to do

Talkative Tony
Easily strikes up conversation with strangers; is often the life of the party

Quiet Quinn
Has trouble thinking of something to say when he meets new people; some think he's unfriendly

Risk-taker Rita
Makes herself vulnerable to have better conversations and expects others to be completely transparent

Risk-avoider Ruth
Wants to avoid looking stupid or admitting she doesn't know things so says as little as possible

There are many other examples of conversation styles. Most people find themselves toward one side or the other. Remembering this is a continuum reminds us we can slide toward the style that would be most helpful in a particular situation.

Style, Substance, and Setbacks

When Conversations Go Wrong, It's Often a Matter of Style

When conversations go wrong, the problem can be a matter of conversational style. Here's something a colleague shared with me. She overheard two coworkers having the following conversation:

A: Hey, should we go to lunch on Friday like we did last week?
B: Yes. Sounds good.
A: Where do you want to go?
B: You liked that taco place. Let's go there.
A: Are you sure? Is there somewhere you want to go instead?
B: The taco place is fine.
A: But I chose last time. What do you feel like?
B: I don't care. Wherever you want is fine.
A: Don't you even want to go?

This is not a very important conversation, but both people ended up feeling frustrated and awkward. What went wrong? Person A reported that she had repeatedly tried to start a conversation to decide together where to go to lunch. She kept trying to get the conversation started, and from her perspective, person B kept shutting it down. On the other hand, person B reported that she had simply answered a question and then had to keep answering it. If person A didn't want an answer, then why did she keep asking questions? In this conversation, Person A is less direct and asks questions as a way to get the conversation started. Person B is more direct, answering the questions and not realizing that person A is looking for a conversation instead of an answer.

It's not a question of right and wrong. It's just a mismatch. Neither person recognizes a style problem, and neither one knows what to do to save the conversation. Take a look at Monica's story.

Case Study: Monica's Story

Monica does everything quickly and loudly. She makes decisions quickly. She asks questions quickly. She answers questions quickly. It's her default style. Most of her team is used to it, and it doesn't bother them. But Kelly is new, and Monica's volume and pace make Kelly really nervous. Kelly likes to take time to consider all her options. She's a good worker, but she doesn't do or say anything to call attention to herself. She likes work, but she has to admit she's a little afraid of Monica. One afternoon, Tom asked Kelly to help him with a last-minute project. Kelly agreed and called Monica to say she'd be working on Tom's project and would be late to the afternoon meeting. Monica wasn't there, so Kelly left a message.

Monica didn't pick up messages before the meeting. When Kelly came in late, Monica interrupted the person who was speaking and (loudly) asked Kelly why she was late and why she hadn't let Monica know. Monica then told everyone that their attendance was expected at these meetings unless they checked in ahead of time. Caught completely off guard, Kelly stood there, head down, cheeks burning, eyes stinging. She mumbled that she was sorry and hurried to take a seat as far from Monica as possible. Kelly didn't raise her eyes the entire meeting.

A couple of hours later, Monica picked up her messages and realized Kelly had called her before the meeting. Monica raced down the hall to Kelly's desk and asked (loudly) why Kelly hadn't told her about the call. Monica expected Kelly to keep her up to date on things like that. Kelly worked in a public space, and she knew everyone was now hearing that she had messed up again. Monica apologized for what she said in the meeting, but her tone, pace, and volume didn't feel like an apology to Kelly.

Head down again, cheeks burning again, Kelly could only nod when Monica asked her to speak up next time.

Kelly is a good worker, and that's one of the reasons Tom reached out to her to help with the last-minute submission. Monica's fast-paced, loud, direct approach makes Kelly so nervous that she freezes and can't do her best work, or even think clearly, around Monica. Monica assumes Kelly doesn't understand the directions, so Monica explains again—and her speed and volume usually increase the second time. Kelly pulls back even more. The harder Monica and Kelly try to communicate, the worse they feel. The problem isn't that they aren't trying. The problem is conversational style.

Recognizing the role that conversational style plays can make a big difference. My client Susan couldn't figure out why she often felt off when speaking with her supervisor. Susan understood what her supervisor wanted her to do, but when they talked about it, Susan ended up feeling defensive and like she'd been put down. She shared the following example with me. When Susan came into work one Monday morning, she saw that the marketing team had left some computer equipment from a weekend meeting in the conference room. Susan called the marketing manager, who was out of the office. The manager asked Susan if she would please put the equipment away. Susan was happy to help. But when Susan's supervisor found out, she was unhappy with Susan. According to the supervisor, Susan should have stood up to the marketing manager and not pitched in. According to her supervisor, Susan's actions created the impression that Susan and her department were less important than the marketing department. Susan was stunned. She thought she was helping—not that she was doing something that diminished her professional standing.

Susan tends to be a collaborative communicator. Her supervisor is a competitive communicator. The supervisor approaches conversations as opportunities to come out ahead. She saw Susan's offer to help another department as a loss in a power struggle. Susan saw it as an opportunity to build a connection. Susan saw this style difference in their other conversations as well. Susan and her supervisor met once a week to review priorities and to set Susan's schedule. The supervisor tended to deliver information by comparing Susan with others and by emphasizing what Susan should do differently in a tone that made Susan feel defensive. Susan felt like she was always being put down.

Once Susan started seeing this as a matter of style instead of constant criticism, she was able to respond in more positive ways. Instead of becoming defensive or feeling like she was being put down, she started focusing on specific requests and recommendations. She also began taking more initiative in bringing things up with her supervisor, subtly reinforcing her credibility. She expressed more appreciation for her supervisor's support and encouragement. Susan has learned how to adapt to her supervisor's style and now feels empowered by their weekly reviews.

Natural Styles

The more you understand another person's natural style, the more effectively you can communicate.

Start by being quiet and watching other people. See how they start conversations. Are they quick to start speaking? Or do they tend to wait for others? Do they speak up in a meeting whenever there's a quiet moment? Or would they rather take time to think through their responses before they say anything?

See how others like to deliver information. Do they get right to the point? Or do they spend some time setting the stage before getting to their points? Do they seem comfortable delivering bad news? Are they so abrupt with bad news that they tend to put people off? Or are they so concerned about sugarcoating bad news that other people can't figure out what's really going on? How do people respond to bad news? Do they become defensive? Do they appreciate feedback? Do they become discouraged and withdraw from the conversation?

As you observe, remind yourself not to judge. Don't compare your style to others' styles and decide that if everyone would simply follow your lead, the world would be a better place. Your goal is to understand others, not to challenge or to change them.

Then, with that mind-set, pay attention to your own style and be objective about it. It's helpful to look at the style you tend to use most often. The best way to assess yourself as a communicator is to ask yourself some specific questions and be completely honest with yourself. Start with these:

- When someone tells you bad news, do you want the person to get right to the point, or do you prefer people to talk about something else for a while so you can prepare to hear something bad?
- When someone criticizes your work, do you welcome the feedback, or do you feel like you want to defend yourself?
- Do you just say whatever pops into your head, or do you think things through so that what you say comes out the way you want it to?
- Is it easy for you to start conversations with new people?
- Do you look forward to having conversations, or would you rather text or email than speak with someone?
- How do you like to gather information? From one source? Many sources? Reading? Discussion? How do you like to share information? Via a phone call? Having a conversation in person? Sending an email or a text message?
- What do you feel when you meet new people? Excitement? Anxiety? Enjoyment? Frustration?
- How do you respond when you are challenged? Do you defend yourself? Assume you are right? Assume the other person is right?

To get helpful information, invite friends and colleagues to share their impressions of you as a communicator. Let them know honest answers will help you understand your style and decide when it's mostly likely to work and when a bit of modification would help. Start with questions like these:

- When we have a conversation, do I get right to the point or chat for a while first?
- Do I ever seem impatient when we're talking?
- Do I talk more about facts or about feelings?
- Do you ever wonder if I'm really listening?
- Do I seem comfortable around new people?
- Do I seem more emotional or analytical when I'm faced with a problem or a disagreement?

Strong observation skills are your friend here! Observe yourself, and ask others to observe you. With this information, you can start thinking about ways you can use style to have better conversations. You can think about different styles and start asking which styles seem to work best with which people. Now you are getting somewhere.

Ways Style Can Work for You

Using a Complementary Style

As you learn more about your own style and the styles of others, you'll notice that flexibility in the way you conduct conversations is a surefire way to become a more effective communicator. When you observe what makes others feel most comfortable and successful, it will help you be successful with them.

You can adapt the style that will increase your connection with a particular person. For example, you can slow down with someone who likes to think before he speaks. Remind yourself not to jump in the moment he stops talking. Give him a few moments to speak. Slow yourself down to match his pace. As he feels more comfortable, he'll likely be able to connect more effectively with you.

You can be careful not to interrupt people who pause regularly in their speaking. If you are someone with a fast speaking style, you probably like to jump in quickly whenever there's a break. But if the other person is still working on expressing her thoughts, this will feel like an interruption to her. And the more often you do it, the more frustrated she might become. In this kind of situation, matching your pace to that of the other person will work better than your usual fast speaking style.

With conversational style, one size definitely does not fit all! The more flexible you can be with your style, the more successful you can be in your conversations.

You can also adjust your style if you are the one with the naturally slower pace. If you prefer to think before you speak and need a few moments to compose your thoughts, you can feel bowled over when trying to have a conversation with someone who drives her conversation in the fast lane. Do your best to match her pace. If you are not finished and need a moment, ask for it—don't assume she'll know to wait for you to finish. Try to speak more firmly whenever you can, and if she seems to be rushing in on top of you, you can try a joking "Oops, let me finish" and then keep speaking.

If you've noticed someone has a hard time hearing bad news, take that into account if you need to deliver some. The bad news needs to be delivered. But think about speaking more slowly and more quietly with someone whom you feel might have a hard time accepting the news. Don't rush through your delivery of bad news to help yourself get it over with as quickly as possible. Helping the other person process the news, recognizing the difficulty involved in the situation, and taking extra time can help people hear and accept bad news.

There are many ways you can change your style to be more effective. My favorite example of this is my friend Shawna. In a large organization, Shawna is the person everyone wants on the team, the person everyone turns to with a problem, and the person managers and employees want to emulate. Part of what people admire and respect about Shawna is her extraordinary expertise and talent. And part of her appeal is her ability to communicate effectively with everyone. She can be confident and direct with some people, slow and careful with others. She seems to sense intuitively which style will work best in a particular conversation. That ability has made Shawna an invaluable member of the organization, and she is the go-to person whenever there's important work to be done.

If you match your style to the style of those in the conversation with you, you'll be amazed at how much more effective everyone in your conversations will be.

Speaking Up in Difficult Situations

We've been looking at personal conversations between a couple of people or among people in small groups. But style can also help in conversations in large groups of people.

I often have people ask me how they can get others to listen to them when they speak in meetings. It's a common question: "When I bring up a point or make a suggestion, no one pays attention. How can I get people to pay attention to me?"

One thing that helps is recognizing that the same approach isn't always effective. In other words, not all meetings have the same culture, and the same style won't always work. Understanding what works with this group in this situation can help you deliver your message in a more effective way.

I had a client who served on the leadership board of a small nonprofit organization. She enjoyed the service, but she hated the board meetings. She worked hard to develop valuable ideas and suggestions, but she couldn't get anyone to pay attention to them at the meetings. I asked her to describe the people who were able to capture people's attention at her board meetings. She realized that these people had a couple of things in common. First, they all seemed to mention the history of the organization and how their ideas fit into the long-term picture of the organization. In addition, instead of getting right to the point, these folks always gave quite a bit of context about their suggestions. In other words, their suggestions were always preceded by some history and some context.

My client, on the other hand, was very nervous whenever she was speaking to this group. She tended to get right to the point and to use as few words as possible. We sometimes think of those who get right to the point as confident and assertive, but that wasn't the case here. The members of the group expected to hear more from those who were making suggestions—they wanted to hear how things fit into the overall history of the organization and to hear about other factors involved. My client's brief suggestions didn't fit that style. So she did her homework. She read about the history of the topic she wanted to address and learned that her idea fit right into the original mission of the organization. She also prepared herself to talk about the reasons for her suggestion and the benefits that her suggestion would offer members of the organization. Prepared in this way, she was able to deliver her comments in the style that worked best for that particular group of people. That effort paid off, and her suggestion was implemented. The content of her suggestion hadn't changed at all; adopting a delivery style that worked for that group helped her succeed.

Being Effective in Groups

When you see people who are successful in conversations that take place in large groups of people, you can pay attention to the speakers' styles. How do they come up with something to say when they are networking? As you pay attention, you might notice that some people research the organization and start their conversations by presenting that information. You might see others who start a conversation with a compliment. Others will start by asking people questions. What can you learn from these successful networkers that would work for you?

One thing you'll probably notice in all different kinds of public conversations is that people who are successful seem genuinely happy to be there. They are smiling. Their gestures are open. They make friendly eye contact. They walk up to other people and greet them. They listen to others and pay attention to them. This friendly, open, attentive style tends to put people around them at ease.

People naturally imitate others when it comes to styles of clothing or accessories. When you see someone wearing an outfit or jewelry that you admire, you might consider wearing something like that yourself. When celebrities are spotted in a particular dress or with a new handbag, that item often sells out in stores. You can do something similar with your conversational style. You can see what works with others as they have conversations in large groups of people, and you can try a similar approach. Pay attention to what works, and see what you can do to incorporate those style choices in your own way in your conversations.

Style, the way we deliver information, can be the thing that helps others focus on the messages we want to deliver. Style is usually developed naturally and used naturally. Sometimes we're not consciously aware of our own style or of the disconnect between our style and the style of others. We just know that something in our conversation is not working. Paying attention to conversational style enables you to make adjustments in the way you share information so you can reduce some of the disconnected feelings. Using the most effective conversational style will help you build strong relationships.

When dealing with people, remember you are not dealing
with creatures of logic, but creatures of emotion.
—Dale Carnegie

CHAPTER 5

SOLVING PROBLEMS AND CREATING SOLUTIONS

What will support any relationship is clear, complete, and
conscious conversations when upsets or breakdowns occur.
—Iyanla Vanzant

Sometimes there are conversations that are really hard to have. Have
you ever needed to talk to someone about something, but you were
uncomfortable bringing it up? Maybe the neighbor's dog barks all
night. Or your coworker plays her music so loudly that you can't
focus on your work. Or your supervisor blamed you for something
that didn't have anything to do with you, and you want to clear up
the matter. Or maybe your child has been spending too much time
on social media with friends and his grades are starting to slip.

Hallmarks of Tough Conversations

Some conversations are just tough. You want to be a good neighbor,
but you need to get some sleep. You want to be a fun coworker and
keep things friendly at the office, but you can't get any work done.
You don't want to appear defensive or throw someone else under the
bus, but you need to stand up for yourself with your supervisor. You

appreciate all the good things about your son, but you need him to get his grades up.

What makes some conversations so tough? Some people make you nervous or have a style that makes you uncomfortable. Some topics are hard to talk about. And some conversations involve a bunch of arguments waiting to happen (some of which you might not be able to anticipate). If there are other people in your life, there will be tough conversations.

What is a tough conversation? A tough conversation is any conversation that, for any reason, presents a difficulty for you or the other person (or other people) involved. And if it's a tough conversation for one person, it'll be a tough conversation for everyone.

Tough doesn't mean terrible. It doesn't mean the relationship is ending. It doesn't have to end in a shouting match. It doesn't even mean all negative. It just means it's hard to have. Speaking to someone who makes you nervous, bringing up a sensitive topic, wondering if you have the complete information, or not knowing how to get the conversation off to a good start can make a conversation tough. You feel nervous, dread the conversation, and just wish you didn't have to have it.

Why have tough conversations? Because they can make things better. And not having them can make things worse. That's what Connie discovered.

Case Study: Connie

Overall, Connie loved her new job. The people were great, and she was doing work that she cared about. She had worried a bit about going to work for a large organization, but the staff there was friendly and the atmosphere was casual and fun. Connie enjoyed sharing an office with Jessica—except for one thing. Connie needed quiet in order to concentrate and get her work done. Jessica played music while she was working. All the time. Loudly.

Connie didn't know what to do. After all, she was the new member of the team, and no one else seemed to mind that Jessica played music at work. People sometimes teased Jessica about her music choices, which they had no trouble hearing from their offices down the hall, but no one ever asked her to turn her music down or turn it off. Connie didn't think she could be the one to ask Jessica to turn down the music. So she didn't say anything. She just kept getting more and more and more frustrated.

One day, when Connie was working on a tough project with a tight deadline, Jessica got so excited about one of the songs she was playing that she started singing along.

Connie snapped. "Are you serious? Now you are singing too? You must be kidding me. Don't you have any sense of what makes a professional space? We are not on Broadway here. This is an office. Enough with the musical theater!"

Shocked, Jessica stopped singing and turned off the music. After that, Connie and Jessica spoke to each other only when absolutely necessary. There was a great deal of tension in the work group, and Connie never felt able to get past the outburst. Eventually, she asked to be transferred to another division.

Connie had felt like asking Jessica to turn down the music would be too hard, but having that tough conversation would have avoided the shouting. It would have been better to have the awkward conversation of asking a coworker to turn down the music or to figure out a way to make things work for both of them than to just simmer and finally explode.

Out of the Frying Pan

Is it always best to just take a breath and have a tough conversation? Not always. Some conversations are worth having, and others are not.

You Need to Decide Which Conversations to Have

How do you decide which conversations to have? Think about the outcome you want and decide which conversations are most likely to make things better for you and the others involved.

Which conversations are worth the effort? Take a look at these three case studies.

Test Case 1: Connor

For three weeks, I was the point person on two proposals. I asked for help, but I never seemed to get it. So a few colleagues and I worked late night after night, and we got both proposals done and delivered. My boss thanked me personally. But when it came time for the department briefing, in front of the whole division, my boss's report didn't mention me or my team at all. My boss just said the proposals were turned in and that she was working on clarifications because there were some errors. It was like all that extra work didn't matter. All that mattered were three or four small mistakes—and her taking the credit for fixing them. I might as well have stayed home or something.

Test Case 2: Ellie

When our department was reorganized, I was promoted. I was really excited and quickly got to work on creating a new work plan and a staffing plan that would be necessary to get the work done. My manager kept saying he was working on getting new staffing approved, so I moved forward. Then, in a budget meeting, my manager announced that our department's staff was all set, and we wouldn't need any additional personnel. His budget for the year was based on the current staff. That was how I found out I wouldn't get the additional people I had been counting on. I feel like I was blindsided, finding out like that in the meeting with everyone there.

Test Case 3: Cassandra

After college, I moved to Seattle and didn't know anyone there. I ended up getting referred to someone else at the company who was looking for a roommate. Isabelle and I hardly knew each other when we started sharing the apartment. It was a one-year lease, so I figured it wouldn't be too bad. At first, it was fine. Isabelle and I had different interests, but things were fine. But one night, she started complaining about work. She was really upset at one of the managers, and she thought she could do things better. At one point, she started describing something that I knew wasn't true. In fact, I could have said a few things that made her feel really stupid for misunderstanding what the manager was doing and what that whole department did.

In each case, the person needs to decide if the conversation is likely to lead to a positive outcome. Connor decided that talking about the specific case wouldn't help. But he did meet with his boss later to talk about getting more people involved in projects earlier to make sure the crunch at the end wasn't repeated. Connor spelled out what his team had done. It was a tough conversation for him since he usually waited for his boss to bring things up. But Connor realized that unless he asked for specific changes, such as a new schedule and more people to be involved, things wouldn't change.

In Ellie's case, she decided she was so angry at her supervisor that she needed to have a conversation about the whole thing. Ellie was angry at her supervisor for changing his mind about Ellie's staffing without consulting her. Ellie was also angry that her supervisor announced his decisions on her staffing in a meeting, which didn't give Ellie a chance to be part of the decision before it was announced in front of the rest of the team. Realizing the staffing decision was made, Ellie decided on two goals for the next conversation with her supervisor: (1) discuss a new plan for the workload based on the new staffing and (2) request that she be informed privately and early about decisions that directly affected her. Ellie made a formal request for the meeting since she thought her supervisor would take her more seriously that way. It was definitely tough, but for Ellie, it was worth it.

Cassandra realized that reacting to what her roommate was saying wouldn't lead to a positive outcome. It was a conversation that didn't need to happen. When Cassandra told me about it, she said, "It was tempting to say something that would make her feel stupid, but I realized she'd still be my roommate in the morning." By choosing not to have the conversation, Cassandra preserved the relationship.

Have tough conversations when they are likely to make things better. When they are not likely to help, let it go.

Tough Talk with Yourself

Sometimes you need to start by having a tough conversation with yourself. You can admit to yourself what you really want and what you are willing to do to get it. And then you can decide if what you want is worth your effort. You need to be honest with yourself and figure out what you want most. Do you really want to go for a promotion at work? Do you know what it will take? Are you willing to work the extra hours? Are you willing to take work home? Before you start having conversations with other people, have a really tough conversation with yourself.

This can force you to admit what you are pretending not to know. Once you've admitted it, you can decide how to deal with it. For example, my friend Leslie was stuck in a job she didn't like. She had been excited to get the job, but over time, the projects she was hired to work on became less important and the job evolved into something else that didn't use her skills or appeal to her. She kept saying, "I don't know what to do." Eventually, she admitted to herself that she did know what to do: talk openly with her supervisor.

The supervisor acknowledged the changes and explained that the division's priorities had shifted. In other words, the new responsibilities were now the job. Leslie had a tough conversation with herself to admit that she needed to figure out what to do. She had a tough conversation with her boss to find out what the future would be for her at the job. And now she has the information she needs to decide what to do next. The tough conversations she had with herself and her boss didn't magically solve her job dilemma, but they did give her the information she needs to make a plan for what to do next.

Having a tough conversation with yourself can get you to clarify your thinking and understand yourself better. As you think about what you really want and what you know, you'll be able to make better decisions about how to move forward. You'll see your options in new ways when you have tough conversations with yourself because those conversations bring forth ideas that probably wouldn't occur to you otherwise. When you need to explain yourself to someone who doesn't understand or agree with you, you need to clarify your thinking to do so. Having a conversation with yourself will help you clear up your ideas before you share them with someone else.

The Path to a Better Outcome

Tough Conversations Can Be a Step in Solving Problems

Tough conversations bring difficult subjects out into the open. You can't solve problems without acknowledging them. What gets talked about gets solved. Tough conversations include asking people what they really want (just like you asked yourself). When you ask people what they really want, be prepared to hear things you might not want to hear. You don't need to agree with everything the other person says, and you don't need to do everything the other person wants you to do. But once problems are expressed, once you hear about them, you can start figuring out ways to resolve them.

Tough conversations raise questions that people don't have easy answers for or questions that don't have any answers yet. But knowing what the questions are can be as important as knowing what the answers are. Once you really understand the questions, you can start working on the answers.

Tough conversations allow and invite people to find ways to change. Sometimes people aren't sure how to change until they have the conversation. Tough conversations can provide the opportunity for them to change and let them know the benefits of changing and the results of not changing. As people recognize the impact of their behavior on others, they can become more understanding about why they should change (and what is driving the request that they do so).

Tough conversations invite people to speak truthfully even when it's hard to do so. Having tough conversations can include stripping away all the extra stuff we use to avoid talking about the truth. That can make it easier for everyone to be more truthful, which can open the way to real progress.

Tough conversations encourage you to hear other people's points of view and take other people more seriously. As people share their ideas with you, you might hear something you don't understand or something you disagree with. The more willing you are to listen carefully and try to understand other people's ideas and opinions, the more you will learn from your conversations with them. As you demonstrate your willingness to listen and learn, you demonstrate your willingness to take the ideas of others more seriously. Your attention to their ideas will help them speak more honestly and helpfully.

Tough conversations can uncover ways people can help each other. These conversations often reveal areas where people are struggling or need help. During these kinds of conversations, people often identify areas where they need help in order to be successful. Recognizing where help is needed can make it easier to move forward successfully. See what you think of Jodie's story.

Case Study: Jodie's Story

As a fairly new manager, Jodie was nervous when Kellie was transferred to her team. Kellie was a good worker, but she tended to make really fast decisions on her projects rather than thinking things through. Then when things went in the wrong direction, Kellie got really defensive. This was a small company, and Jodie had seen it happen before.

After a few months, it happened: Kellie made a hasty decision about a hardware purchase, and things didn't work out. As the first debrief approached, Jodie wanted to avoid the defensiveness. She asked herself what she wanted most and realized it was for Kellie to fix the problem without feeling bad about it.

When they met, Jodie asked about the status of the project. Kellie started giving excuses about the delays. Instead of challenging her, Jodie asked, "What can we do right now to make things better? How are you going to get back on track? How will you keep things on schedule from here on out? How can I help?" Questions like those helped them move forward to problem solving. Once they came up with a reasonable approach, Jodie asked how Kellie would keep the same problem from occurring again. This gave Kellie a chance to own her contribution and own her power to change. Using questions and letting Kellie take the lead in finding answers seemed to help her solve the problem.

Jodie's approach included asking the right questions and waiting for Kellie to answer instead of jumping in and telling Kellie what to do. By stepping back and inviting Kellie to share her ideas, Jodie helped Kellie take responsibility for moving things forward.

Preparing for Tough Conversations

Tough conversations take preparation. Whatever makes them difficult means that the stakes are high. Tough conversations matter—and they have the potential to go wrong. Being prepared doesn't guarantee that the conversation will go well, but it will make it more likely that it will go well. Do whatever it takes to be prepared for tough conversations. Learn everything you can.

You can prepare yourself for a tough conversation by practicing what you will need to say in it. Tough conversations might include needing to say something that's difficult for you to say. Practice saying the words out loud. It's important that you become comfortable hearing yourself saying the words. This will help you feel more confident. Try saying them in different ways, saying them over and over until you are completely comfortable with what it feels like to say them and hear them. That will help you stay calm and focused when you're actually in the conversation with other people.

One of my clients was frustrated by her lack of success in interviews. She had great credentials—and she caught the eye of several organizations—but she just couldn't manage to shine in the interview. As she and I talked about it, I realized that she wasn't comfortable talking about her accomplishments. When she heard herself saying how well she had done in school or describing experiences that made her a great candidate for a job, she became so uncomfortable that her voice trailed off and she just stopped. I had her say those things over and over. She needed to be comfortable talking about herself and hearing herself say those things. Until she was comfortable hearing herself say the words, she wasn't able to say them with confidence. Practice helped my client speak about herself in compelling ways. As her confidence increased, she became more successful, and soon, she was offered a great job.

Prepare for success by planning the best place and time for the conversation. Time and space can get in the way—or they can set the stage for a productive conversation. Sometimes people need time to think. Space can also be important. Supervisors who stand behind a large desk and speak down to an employee who is sitting in a small, uncomfortable chair make it harder for that employee to speak up. Where will you both be comfortable and able to speak honestly and freely?

Figure out what's important to the other person or people involved. To be successful, you need to know what matters to other people as well as what matters to you. Do your homework. Find out how people feel about things. Have a preconversation conversation if you need to. As well as learning about the people involved, learn everything you can about the topic. The more you know, the more prepared you'll be to respond appropriately.

You might need to do some preparing even while you are partway through the conversation. If a conversation becomes tough or takes an unexpected turn and you need some time to gather your thoughts and to prepare for whatever is coming, then ask for it. Call an audible and take a break.

Think about the way you say things. Denying a request can be tough, so think about what will most likely lead to success. Sometimes a short answer is most effective. For example, when a theater staged a student festival, the staff decided to reserve orchestra seating for students and have parents sit upstairs in the balcony.

Many parents wanted to sit in the orchestra. When the staff members gave lengthy answers and tried to explain how there wasn't enough seating for all the parents and the staff couldn't make exceptions for some parents and not others, the staff members seemed to be inviting debate. When they simply said, "Parents sit upstairs" and left it at that, there was less pushback. The way you say things, especially when you are saying no, can have a big effect on the way others hear the information. Being straightforward and brief can make a tough conversation less difficult.

Prepare yourself to stay on track despite how the other person in your conversation responds. You can prepare for possible responses, but you also need to expect the unexpected. Tough conversations often go in directions that are unpredictable. Remember that not everything will go as planned—and people might not speak or act as you would expect them to. Whatever the other person says, you get to choose your response. Sometimes, you can steer the conversation in ways that avoid potential problems. For example, if you know there is a chance that a conversation with a family member will end up in a heated discussion about your political differences, you can plan to say, "Tell me more about your work" or "What's the latest on your renovation plans?" at the first sign of trouble. Making a commitment to keep the conversation on friendly turf and keeping the conversation out of the danger zone can protect the relationship. Control what you can.

Focusing on the Positive Outcome

It's tempting to avoid tough conversations or, when we can't avoid them, to get through them as quickly as possible. A better approach is to focus on what positive outcomes can come out of the conversation.

You can plan ways to keep the positive outcome in mind when things get really tough. What is the good outcome you want? Ask yourself, "What do I want to be true after the conversation?" What can you do and say to move closer to that outcome? If things start going in the wrong direction, remember to have a strategy for a pause button if necessary. You'll feel better if you know there's a way to slow things down if you need to. Keep yourself focused on the positive outcome, and keep yourself moving toward that.

Frame as much of your thinking and your approach as possible toward a positive outcome—even when it's not obvious. For example, letting an employee go because he's not a good fit is a step to his finding a job where he can truly succeed. You've already identified the benefit to you in letting him go, but think about how letting him go can help him as well. Of course, you need to be sincere if you express this. An offhanded remark like "Actually, I'm really doing you a favor here" is unlikely to help. Being sincere about what's best for both of you can help.

If the tough part is saying no when the other person really wants a yes, see if there is something positive that you can offer. I learned this lesson from my mom years ago. A community group arranged daily help for a neighbor whose health was failing. The person in charge asked my mom to participate. Although she wanted to help, her work schedule meant she couldn't come in once a week. There was something she could do, however, and that was to organize the help team. My mom kept the schedule, found replacements when someone was unable to come at the last minute, and made sure everything ran smoothly. She couldn't say yes to the initial request, but she found a way she could be involved. Find your yes.

Keeping your mind on the positive outcome can help you be more curious and increase your understanding. You know where you want to end up, so how can you get there? How can you use this conversation, tough as it might be, to make progress? What can you learn from the other person that will get you there? Understanding where someone else is coming from is necessary if you are going to make progress together.

Sometimes we need to take a step back to figure out what that positive outcome really is. Several years ago, a friend shared a humorous exchange between her husband and her son. She took a class one night a week, and that night, Dad was in charge of dinner. Here is how one of the dinnertime conversations went between the father and his son:

Dad: Eat your peas.
Son: No. Peas are gross.
Dad: Peas are not gross. They are healthy. Eat up.
Son: No.
Dad: Seriously, no dessert unless you eat those peas.
Son: No. They are gross. I don't want dessert.
Dad: Eat your peas or you are not getting up from the table.
Son: I want Mom.

As you can imagine, the situation deteriorated pretty quickly after this exchange between the dad and his son. It's easy to think that the young boy and his dad had two very different outcomes in mind: one involving eating peas and one involving absolutely not eating peas under any circumstances. But what do they really want? Dad wants a healthy son. He wants his son to develop healthy eating habits, and that means eating green vegetables. He wants his son to grow up strong and healthy. And what does the son want? He wants a sense of independence. He's too small and too young to be in charge of much, and at four years old, he's frustrated by that. He's busy becoming his own person, and he wants to make decisions himself. He wants to practice choosing, and he wants to do that with dinner.

But the son also wants to be strong and healthy. And the dad also wants his son to practice making choices. Being healthy and strong includes being able to make choices. So, yes, vegetables. But do they have to be peas? What if the son could be involved in choosing which vegetables to have for dinner and how to prepare them? What about beans? Or even a salad now and then? The positive outcomes that the dad and the son desire are actually pretty close. If they (well, at least the dad) can keep their positive outcomes in mind, then there's a much better chance of having a fun family dinner instead of tears.

Here are some ways to keep your eyes on that positive outcome prize:

- Be careful about your questions and your responses to questions. Be curious about the other person, not challenging. Acknowledging that you don't know what the other person is thinking or feeling gives you an opportunity to learn. Try to learn. Help the other person learn from you as well. Don't be defensive when you are asked questions. Share what you know.
- Think positively about the other person. Try to learn from other ideas, even when you don't agree with them. Look for areas of new knowledge and even areas of agreement.
- Remember the power of aligning your ideas with your conversation partner's ideas. It's not always easy, and it might not work in exactly the way you expected. Working for positive outcomes opens up all kinds of possibilities.

Focusing on a positive outcome, or just on the possibility of a positive outcome, can inspire you to initiate a tough conversation. Consider Olivia's story.

Case Study: Olivia's Story

One of Olivia's tough conversations was initiated by an employee. Keith was one of those transfers who wouldn't stop talking about how great things were at his last assignment and questioning the new team's approach. At one point, he gave Olivia a bunch of advice about how she should handle a particular situation. Olivia was frustrated and told Keith firmly that she would handle it. About a month later, he called and asked if they could have lunch. Olivia was hesitant but agreed. Keith started off by saying he was sorry that things had gotten off on the wrong foot. He admitted he had spoken before he understood what was going on. He asked for a second chance. It was a good move on his part. Olivia gave him a second chance, and things have worked out well. That conversation made the difference in turning the relationship around.

Olivia's example shows someone who saw the possibility of a positive outcome and was willing to take a chance. Focusing on the positive outcome provided an opportunity for two colleagues to start over—something they are both glad to have.

Taking Steps to Be Successful: Step Up, Step Back, and Step Away

When you have identified the positive outcome and prepared for the tough conversation, there are three basic steps to keep in mind to have successful tough conversations: step up, step back, and step away.

Step 1: Step Up

Review the situation. Make a plan. Learn all you can. Remember that problems don't usually solve themselves—they usually get worse.

Start in a positive way. Share your ideas about the positive outcome. Assume you will get there. Speak as if you are on your way there. Invite the other person to work with you to get there.

Be straightforward about what you want. Be clear. Be polite and friendly and get to the point.

Step 2: Step Back

Let the other person talk. It's not a conversation if only one person talks. In a tough conversation, it's especially important that people are invited to speak. Ask questions and be curious about the answers. Really listen. Try to understand people, especially when you don't agree with them.

Get comfortable with silence. Don't rush the other person. Give her time to think. Don't rush in and simply answer your own questions or move on. Just let there be a little silence.

Move the conversation forward when you are not the one speaking. The way to do this is to demonstrate your support of the speaker by smiling, leaning in, and having friendly, open body language.

Step 3: Step Away

Know when to end the conversation. You have limits; know what you're not willing to talk about. Other people have limits too. Pay attention to when they seem to be reaching the limit. Sometimes a conversation stops being productive. Know when to take a break and when to continue. Know when the topic has been covered enough for this conversation. Don't make the decision about fault. Don't say, "Well, I can't talk to you when you get like this." Make the decision about what's most likely to get you to that positive outcome: "I think we'll have a better conversation if we take a break for a little while."

Make clear if it is a break or an end. If you will pick up the conversation, agree about when and how.

Recognize that the other person won't necessarily agree with your decision to take a break. Work with the other person to create an agreement. Involve the other person in planning what comes next.

Being Realistic about Emotions

People tend to become emotional during tough conversations. Even when we start out calmly, tough conversations can make us feel vulnerable or threatened or angry. When feelings get involved, it's more difficult to remain calm.

Emotions make it more difficult to behave well and speak carefully. Emotions can be like the wake that's left behind after a boat speeds by. The speeding boat is long gone but the resulting troubled water causes the other boats to bump up against each other and against the pier. Your emotions might not last, but if you allow them to speed through the conversation, the resulting words might cause damage that you didn't anticipate.

That doesn't mean you should attempt to banish your emotions. You can't. You can't pretend to park your emotions at the curb, and it won't be helpful to say, "No need to get angry" or "You shouldn't feel that way" to yourself or to someone else. People feel things; that's part of what we do. We feel. We have emotions.

Instead of denying or burying emotions, you can manage them. If you feel yourself getting upset, you can slow down. Literally slow down. Take two deep breaths instead of one. Speak more slowly. If you are making gestures, you can make them more slowly. Slowing yourself down can help you manage your feelings so they don't manage you.

If you sense the other person is getting upset, you can suggest taking a break, using language that is designed to help the other person relax. Try saying, "I think I'd like a bit of time to think more about all of this. I'd like to take a break." Don't accuse someone else of getting out of control. Simply ask for a break.

Recognize that the other person might speak from an emotion and might say something that challenges or insults you. You might be tempted to respond in kind. You might think of a brilliantly insulting response—and you might want to deliver this response in order to feel superior to your conversation partner. Don't. Don't speak from your own emotions. Don't speak from the other person's emotions (even if the other person does). Control what you say.

With children, parents and teachers often say, "If you can't think of something nice to say, don't say anything." Sometimes not saying anything is exactly the right choice. There's nothing wrong with a moment of silence. If someone says something that's not productive, you don't need to respond in kind. You can choose not to respond—and then you can enjoy the silence. It means you have overcome the temptation to say the wrong thing at the tempting moment.

Pay attention to your emotions. Figure out what is behind them. Why do you feel this way? As the famous film critic Roger Ebert said, "Your emotions will never lie to you."[23] Acknowledge your emotions and resolve them, but do not invite them to tough conversations.

Taking Responsibility for What Comes Next

Tough conversations often end up in unexpected ways. That can leave one or all participants wondering about what comes next.

That next phase often determines the long-term, lasting impact of the conversation.

If things went badly in a tough conversation, careful follow-up can reassure people and reestablish a productive relationship. I once chastised an employee for an error she had made. The employee had done something wrong, and I was right to talk to her about it. However, I should not have spoken to her the way I did. I spoke in anger instead of waiting until I had calmed down. I discounted what she said to explain her decision. I was completely in the wrong.

Afterward, I felt terrible—and I bet she did too. I needed to make things right. I made an appointment to see her and apologized to her. I talked about my bad behavior (I did not talk about her error; that wasn't part of this conversation). I told her I was wrong and hoped she could forgive me. I went out of my way to greet her warmly and with appreciation the next several times we met. I had taken the original conversation in a completely wrong direction, and it was my responsibility to make things right. Fortunately, she was a very good sport about it, and we have maintained a good working relationship ever since.

If a conversation uncovered new ground, you can follow up to see what can be learned. Tough conversations can push people to think in new ways. I have a colleague who reported a tough conversation with a manager of another division after a space was double-booked. My colleague and her team showed up to set up the room before the previous event was over. In the conversation, my colleague realized they had both reserved the space, but they had spoken with different people. After everything was over and settled, my colleague followed up with the facilities manager. It was important to know the appropriate scheduling procedure to avoid repeating the problem.

If you ended up pushing the pause button because emotions threatened to take over, follow up to resume the conversation in more positive ways. Taking a break is a positive move when things take a bad turn, but leaving things hanging can reinforce the bad feelings. When you take the break, set a time to reconnect: "I need a little time to think about this. Let's pick this up tomorrow right after lunch. Does that work for you?" If your first suggestion doesn't work, go back and try again. The longer you wait, the firmer the bad feelings become—and the harder it is to make things right. Don't let a well-timed break turn into something that breaks up the relationship.

Use Your Charm

No matter how the tough conversation ended, express your appreciation to the other people included. Thank people for their time and effort. Whatever the final outcome of the conversation, however tough it has been for you, thank the other people involved for their time and effort. Everyone is busy, and everyone appreciates a sincere thank-you. Offer that. Remember that tough conversations can be used to make things better. Even if you don't resolve disagreements—and even if the final result is an agreement to end a relationship—there's no benefit to ongoing bad feelings. Even disagreements should end as positively as possible. Expressing appreciation is a good way to end a tough conversation on a positive note.

There is a great line in the movie *What's Up, Doc?* (Actually, there are so many great lines in that movie that I've lost count of them.) In the movie, some thieves want to take jewels from a rich hotel guest. The thieves need someone to distract the rich hotel guest so she won't go back to the room while they are searching for the jewels. The boss assigns one of his helpers to delay her so the others can break into the room. When the helper asks his boss how he should prevent the hotel guest from returning to her room, the boss says, "Use your charm."[24]

When navigating the ever-tricky waters of tough conversations, that advice comes in handy. Use your charm. In addition to any personal charisma you might have, you can try these strategies:

C: Control yourself—all your words and actions.
H: Help others in any way you can.
A: Act quickly—the longer you put things off, the harder it gets.
R: Respect others and their opinions and let them know that you respect them.
M: Move forward.

Use your charm—and have the tough conversations that will lead you to success.

Having Conversations That Strengthen and Heal Relationships

Remember that any conversation could be the one that changes everything. Most conversations make some difference in your relationships. Some conversations make more of a difference than others. Some conversations have very little impact. Any conversation, however, could be the one that makes a huge difference. You never know which conversation could be the one that changes everything. Treat each conversation as having that potential, and each conversation can make a relationship stronger.

Of course, having people in your life means having relationships that get off track. If something has gone wrong in a relationship, conversations can help get things back on track.

The following are kinds of conversations that can strengthen and heal relationships:

- Honest conversations where we say what we think but remember to be kind to other people and make a conscious effort not to hurt them.
- Generous conversations that are focused on other people's needs as well as our own.
- Brave conversations that are opportunities to take responsibility for mistakes and misunderstandings and to make things better.
- Growth-oriented conversations that may start small, with ordinary topics, but grow into something more significant in which we talk about things that matter.
- Engaged conversations where we listen with the intent of understanding and make it easy for others to understand us.

- Balanced conversations where people disagree but continue to respect other people and other views.
- Shared conversations where everyone has a chance to be in the spotlight.

Having healing conversations can restore a relationship when things have gone wrong. Apologizing and taking responsibility for what has gone wrong and for what needs to be done in the future is a way to use a healing conversation to make a relationship stronger than before. These steps can be helpful.

- *Being in learning mode.* Healing conversations often uncover information that is new or unexpected, as well as information that is unwelcome. Healing conversations need curiosity, not defensiveness, to do their work.
- *Taking responsibility for your words, your actions, and their impact.* Healing conversations recognize that people make mistakes and require that they take responsibility for those mistakes.
- *Controlling what you say.* Healing conversations mean that you don't act out, don't speak every idea that wanders across your mind, and don't say the tempting thing at the tempting moment. Healing conversations require that you control yourself and that you do not attempt to score points by putting someone down or by making a victory out of someone's mistake.
- *Being honest—even when it's hard.* Healing conversations require honesty, even when the honest answer is hard to hear. Healing conversations are honest, even when the honest answer is "I don't know." Healing conversations build on honesty to increase understanding. These conversations require that you be honest with yourself and with others.

Healing conversations require that you answer the question "What am I pretending not to know?"

- *Committing to the other person and to the relationship.* Healing conversations are not just two people talking at each other. Healing conversations require more. They require interaction, engagement, and involvement.

When people struggle, conversations can help. When relationships are damaged, conversations can help. When people feel awkward or uncomfortable, conversations can help. Conversations can help a friend or a relative in need.

When in doubt, have a conversation.

If you are trying to take a difficult decision and you're weighing up the pros and cons, you have frank conversations. Everybody knows this in their walk of life.
—Tony Blair

CONCLUSION

GETTING STARTED

Each person's life is lived as a series of conversations.
—Deborah Tannen

If you walk a few blocks in any large city, you'll see an amazing collection of people doing all kinds of things—business executives making deals, neighbors cleaning up a park, parents and teachers helping children learn and play, artists displaying masterpieces, designers displaying jewelry and outfits, musicians performing, and volunteers making the world a better place. Everywhere you look, there are people pursuing their interests and dreams and doing what they need to do to succeed.

With all the people I've worked with, success is tied up with relationships. People work with vendors and colleagues and clients and supervisors. People have fun with family and friends and neighbors. Success in work and in life comes largely from our relationships. And strong, meaningful relationships are built over time—in large part through conversations.

Most people associate their success, the best parts of their personal and professional lives, with the people who share their lives. Building those relationships, then, is the work we do to achieve success. And having great conversations is one of the ways we consistently build and strengthen relationships.

Here are some practical (and fun!) ways to incorporate these ideas into your everyday conversations.

Making Relationships a Top Priority

- Think about the most important people in your personal life and your professional life. Consider your relationship with each one of them. Do you dedicate enough time and energy to maintain and strengthen these relationships?
- Do a time assessment of the last week. How often have you spent high-quality time (you can define high-quality time for yourself, but be honest—sitting next to someone while you are both texting other people isn't really high-quality time) with the people you just identified as important to you?
- Choose three people you could help or strengthen or serve by reaching out. Then ... reach out! Make a phone call. Set up a lunch. Plan an outing. Over the next ten days, make a conscious effort to serve or help someone in a personal way.
- Think about a relationship that you have let go stale. Perhaps it's a friend who moved away or a family member who doesn't often come to reunions or a coworker who left for another job. Reach out to that person. Don't ask for anything—just reach out and say hello. Reconnect and reinvigorate the relationship.
- Okay, here is the hard one. Think of a relationship in your life that needs CPR. Perhaps you had an argument and allowed bad feelings to remain, criticized someone and didn't apologize, or just never made the effort to get past an initial negative impression. Go up to that person and smile and say something nice. Say something that takes some effort on your part and is genuine and true. Don't expect anything in return—act in kindness and then accept whatever happens.

Choosing the Best Conversation to Have

- Think about a conversation you have been meaning to have but haven't gotten around to yet. Perhaps you keep meaning to thank another parent for driving your child home from swim practice or you wish you could think of something to say to make the new neighbor feel welcome or you really need to ask your supervisor for a raise. Write out five reasons why you have been procrastinating. Then write out five benefits of having the conversation. Choose which matters most to you.

- During conversations with someone who makes you uncomfortable, make a conscious, ongoing effort to look for positive attributes about the person. Choose to focus on positive things instead of negative things.

- When you see people who make different decisions than you do, remind yourself that there are many ways to live a happy and successful life. Ask people questions about their decisions to learn more about them.

- Plan to have a positive outcome in your conversations. The more worrisome the conversation, the more you can benefit from expecting and working toward a good outcome. Spend time imagining the best possible outcome and think of different ways to get there.

- Whenever you think "I don't know how to," "I can't," or "This won't work," choose different language. Take responsibility for making things work out.

Listening and Understanding Your Way to Success

- Carefully monitor how much you talk when you're with family and friends. Observe your talk-to-listen ration. Then increase how much you listen. Start with family and friends, where it's easier to develop a habit of listening.

- After you've practiced with family and friends, increase how much you listen with other people. Try strategies like silently counting to ten before jumping into a conversation or waiting until three other people have spoken before you make another comment.
- Try to learn something from every conversation you have. Set a goal to learn from all the people around you: the drugstore clerk, your child's teacher, your supervisor, the stranger in the elevator, a neighbor, a family member. See how much you can learn from other people every day.
- Think of interesting, friendly, thought-provoking questions you can ask people to get to know them better. When you meet someone, instead of saying, "What do you do?" ask questions that get to what matters to them: "What do you really enjoy doing in your spare time?" or "What's your favorite childhood memory?" or "How can I help you meet your goals?" Think about what you wish people would ask you so you could answer in a way that would make you feel interesting. Ask questions like that.
- Listen in ways that are most helpful to the different styles around you. With quiet people, listen more quietly and give them time to think. With talkative people, try asking more questions. Take your cue from others, and help them share ideas.

Exploring Style and Making Connections

- Pay attention to your own speaking style. Are you a direct and bottom-line-up-front person? Do you seek consensus before moving forward? Are you sometimes hesitant about joining a conversation? Do you jump in without really knowing what you are going to say?
- Pay attention to the speaking styles of other people. Who seems to have the easiest time joining a conversation? Who

tends to wait for an invitation? Who is direct or even abrupt? Who takes everyone's feelings into account? Think about the distinct styles of the people around you.

- When a conversation goes unexpectedly wrong, take a quick break to figure out if the problem is with content or style. Do you and the other person actually agree about the topic but still don't feel like you are on the same page? That's an indication that it's probably a style problem.

- When you experience a mismatch in style, make an effort to step back and try to match your style to the other person. If you are more direct and the other person is hesitant, hold back a little. If you are the hesitant one, try to jump in and participate more freely.

- Remember that style is not *right* or *wrong*. It is just *different*. Practice different styles so you can be more effective in your personal and professional relationships.

Solving Problems and Creating Solutions

- Think about a few conversations that made you uncomfortable or didn't work for whatever reasons. Putting emotion or a sense of who is right aside, try to figure out what went wrong. Do you see any patterns in conversations that go wrong?

- Choose one conversation that did not go the way you expected. Reimagine it, and see yourself making different choices. These choices might include saying something different, leaving some things unsaid, asking questions and trying to understand, or even ending the conversation earlier. Focus on yourself and what you could have done to bring it to a better outcome.

- Set up some criteria for which tough conversations you need to have. Then apply those criteria to the tough conversations lurking in your future. Do you need to step back and think before you jump in? Do you need to be more active and stop procrastinating?

- Identify your *triggers*—things that get you emotionally caught up and make you more likely to say or do something you will regret. Have a plan to act in appropriate ways if your trigger comes up in conversation.

- Before, during, and after a tough conversation, focus on the positive outcome. If you cannot imagine a positive outcome, maybe you shouldn't have the conversation. If the positive outcome is getting further away during the conversation, maybe it's time to change direction or stop. If the positive outcome wasn't achieved, what do you need to do next?

What's Next?

Enjoy the great conversations in your life and the strong and meaningful relationships you are cultivating.

And keep in touch! I'd love to hear your story. Share at carolann@carolannlloydstanger.com or @calloydstanger. Let's have a great conversation!

The noblest pleasure is the joy of understanding.
—Leonardo da Vinci

NOTES

[1] Krietzer, Mary Jo. "Why Personal Relationships Are Important." Taking Charge of Your Health & Wellbeing. 2016. Accessed June 15, 2016. https://www.takingcharge.csh.umn.edu/enhance-your-wellbeing/relationships/why-personal-relationships-are-important.

[2] "The Benefits of Heathy Relationships." Positive Psychlopedia. May 2015. Accessed May 15, 2016. https://positivepsychlopedia.com/year-of-happy/the-benefits-of-relationships.

[3] Izadi, Elahe. "Your relationships are just as important to your health as diet and exercise." The Washington Post. January 05, 2016. Accessed June 10, 2016. https://www.washingtonpost.com/news/to-your-health/wp/2016/01/05/your-relationships-are-just-as-important-to-your-health-as-exercising-and-eating-well/?utm_term=.8c433093dd2b.

[4] Publications, Harvard Health. "The health benefits of strong relationships." Harvard Health. Accessed June 10, 2016. http://www.health.harvard.edu/newsletter_article/the-health-benefits-of-strong-relationships.

[5] Gatty, Ann. "The Importance of Healthy Relationships." SelfGrowth.com. Accessed May 1, 2016. http://www.selfgrowth.com/articles/the-importance-of-healthy-relationships.

[6] Schnall, Simone, Kent D. Harber, Jeanine K. Stefanucci, and Dennis R. Proffitt. "Social Support and the Perception of Geographical Slant." Journal of *Experimental Social Psychology*. September 01, 2008. Accessed March 10, 2016. https://www.ncbi.nlm.nih.gov/pmc/articles/PMC3291107.

[7] "5 Hidden Benefits of Being in a Long-Term Relationship." Psychology Today. Accessed March 10, 2016. https://www.psychologytoday.com/blog/in-practice/201504/5-hidden-benefits-being-in-long-term-relationship.

8   Smith, Emily Esfahani. "Relationships Are More Important Than Ambition." *The Atlantic*. April 16, 2013. Accessed May 10, 2016. http://www.theatlantic.com/health/archive/2013/04/relationships-are-more-important-than-ambition/275025.

9   Tarvin, Andrew. "The Importance of Relationships in the Workplace." Humor at Work. Accessed March 10, 2016. http://www.humorthatworks.com/learning/the-importance-of-relationships-in-the-workplace.

10   Laws, Kimberley. "The Importance of Business Relationships | Build a Strong Team." Propel Businessworks. April 28, 2015. Accessed May 15, 2016. http://propelbusinessworks.com/guest-blogs/relationships-matter.

11   Svane, Mikkel. "Beyond Customer Loyalty Programs: 7 Ways To Build Lasting Relationships | Fast Company | The Future Of Business." Fast Company. April 02, 2014. Accessed June 5, 2016. https://www.fastcompany.com/3028477/leadership-now/beyond-customer-loyalty-programs-7-ways-to-build-lasting-relationships.

12   McFarlin, Kate. "Importance of Relationships in the Workplace." Small Business-Chron.com. June 01, 2011. Accessed July 5, 2016. http://smallbusiness.chron.com/importance-relationships-workplace-10380.html.

13   Positano, Dr. Rock. "The Mystery of the Rosetan People." The Huffington Post. November 23, 2007. Accessed March 10, 2016. http://www.huffingtonpost.com/dr-rock-positano/the-mystery-of-the-roseta_b_73260.html.

14   Smith, Emily Esfahani. "Relationships Are More Important Than Ambition." *The Atlantic*. April 16, 2013.

15   Tannen, Deborah. *You Just Don't Understand: Men and Women in Conversation*. New York, NY: William Morrow. 2007.

16   Scott, Susan. *Fierce Conversations*. New York, NY: Penguin Publishing Group. 2004.

17   Covey, Stephen. *The Seven Habits of Highly Effective People*. New York, Simon and Schuster, 1989.

18   Universal Pictures. *Apollo 13*. Directed by Ron Howard. 1995.

19   Kline, John A. *Listening Effectively*. Alabama: Air University Press/Maxwell Air Force Base. 1996.

20   Foster, Nancy. "Good Communication Starts With Listening." Mediate.com - Find Mediators-World's Leading Mediation Information Site. Accessed March 10, 2016. http://www.mediate.com/articles/foster2.cfm.

21   Covey, Stephen. *The Seven Habits of Highly Effective People*.

[22] Fellowes, Julian. *Downton Abbey*. Carnival Film & Television. 2010.
[23] Makarechi, Kia. "Roger Ebert Quotes: Remembering The Wit And Wisdom of a Legend." *The Huffington Post*. April 04, 2013. Accessed July 5, 2016. http://www.huffingtonpost.com/2013/04/04/roger-ebert-quotes_n_3017751.html.
[24] Warner Brothers. *What's Up Doc?* Directed by Peter Bogdonovich. 1972.

INDEX

A

academic success, impact of relationships on, 3–4
alternate routes, in conversations, 31–34
Anne (case study), 16–17
The Atlantic, 5–6

B

Blair, Tony, 102
body language, 46, 56, 57, 95
bridge, building of, 48–51

C

Carnegie, Dale, 78
Carol (case study), 25
case studies
    Anne, 16–17
    Carol, 25
    Connie, 80–81
    Doug, 44–45
    Emily, 33–34
    Janet, 14–15
    Jodie, 87–88
    Judy, 54–55
    Ken, 53–54

Kristin, 34–35
Monica, 69–71
Olivia, 93–94
Penelope, 59–60
Sheri, 48
Tonya, 66–67
Cassandra (test case), 83, 84
charm, use of, 99–100
choice
    of best conversation to have, 105
    of honesty and respect, 37–39
    making of in conversations, 31–34
    of next steps, 39
    power of, 21–24
collaborative communicator, as style, 71
communication style, 67. *See also* conversational style
communicator, assessing yourself as, 73–74
community success, impact of relationships on, 4–6
competitive communicator, as style, 71

complexities, as element of real conversations, 12

connections, making of, xiii, 2, 7, 8, 11–17, 22, 61–78, 106–107

Connie (case study), 80–81

Connor (test case), 82, 83

conversational style, 61, 63, 65–68, 69, 71, 75, 78

conversations
alternate routes in, 31–34
choosing best ones to have, 105
deciding which ones to have, 82–84
defined, 8–9
destinations in, 34–41
direction in, 31–34
doctor-patient conversation, 10–11
effectively ending of, 36
electronic conversations, 8–11
elements of, 12–13
face-to-face conversation, 8, 9, 10, 14, 17
follow-up to, 39, 40–41, 97–98
having ones that strengthen and heal relationships, 100–102
healing conversations, 101–102
honest conversations, 13, 100
impact of technology on, 8–11, 14
live conversations, 21–24
outcomes in, 34–41
phone conversations, 9, 14, 17
power of, 18–19
public conversations, 65, 78
rapport conversations, 7–8
report conversations, 7–8, 9

tough conversations. See tough conversations

tough talk with yourself, 84–85

when they go wrong, 64–65

when to have/when not to have, 24–25

cost, as element of real conversations, 12–13

Covey, Stephen, 32, 60

D

Da Vinci, Leonardo, 109

destinations, in conversations, 34–41

difficult situations, speaking up in, 76–77

Direct Doris, conversational style of, 68

direction, in conversations, 31–34

doctor-patient conversation, 10–11

Doug (case study), 44–46

Downton Abbey (television series), 62

E

Ebert, Roger, 97

Einstein, Albert, 36

electronic conversations, 8–11

Ellie (test case), 82–84

email, 7, 9–10, 14, 21, 22, 23, 57, 73

Emily (case study), 33–34

emotions
being realistic about, 96–97
cautions when emotions are high, 24, 26, 34, 98
keeping some distance from, 21, 31
personal relationships as vulnerable to, 15

expressions, 62–63
eye contact, 56, 57, 78

F

face-to-face conversation, 8, 9, 10,
       14, 17
feedback, 38, 53, 72, 73
follow-up, to conversations, 39,
       40–41, 97–98
Foster, Nancy J., 59
friendships, xi, xii, 3, 4, 15–16, 41

G

goal, as element of real
       conversations, 12, 26–28
groups, being effective in, 77–78

H

healing conversations, 101–102
Hemingway, Ernest, 60
highly interactive listeners, 50
highly receptive listeners, 50
Holt, Lester, 41
honest conversations, 13, 100
honesty
       choosing of, 37–39
       healing conversations as
              requiring, 101

I

IM, 9
image, 62–63
Indirect Isabelle, conversational
       style of, 68

J

Janet (case study), 14–15

Jobs, Steve, 62–63
Jodie (case study), 87–88
The Journal of Applied Psychology, 5
Judy (case study), 54–55
just say no, 32

K

Ken (case study), 53–54
Kranz, Gene, 38
Kristin (case study), 34–35

L

language
       body language, 46, 56, 57, 95
       use of, 46
learning, listening as time for,
       44–46
Lewis, C. S., xi
listening
       benefits of, 49–50, 51, 56,
              59, 60
       as building relationships,
              58–60
       committing to being better at,
              55–57
       demonstrating that you are
              listening, 57–58
       steps for being successful in,
              45–46
       styles of, 50–51
       as time for learning, 44–46
       as way to success, 43–60,
              105–106
live conversations, reasons for,
       21–24

M

mental health, impact of
relationships on, 2–3
Meyer, Joyce, 19
misunderstanding, 12, 15, 48, 64,
66–67, 83, 100
Monica (case study), 69–71

N

natural styles, 67, 72–74
needs, as element of real
conversations, 13
Nevill, Dorothy, 21
Newton, Joseph F., xiii
next steps, choosing of, 39–41

O

Olivia (case study), 93–94
organizational success, impact of
relationships on, 4–6
outcomes. *See also* positive outcome
in conversations, 34–41
focusing on positive outcome,
90–94
path to better outcome, 86–102

P

participatory listeners, 50
Penelope (case study), 59–60
personal connections, building
blocks of, 11–17
personal relationships
admitting hurt feelings in, 41
evolution of, 15–16, 17
perspective, 25–30
phone conversations, 9, 14, 17

phones, importance of putting away
of, 57–58
physical health, impact of
relationships on, 1–2
positive outcome, 34, 83, 84, 90–
91, 92–94, 95, 105, 108
problems, solving of, 79–102,
107–108
professional connections, building
blocks of, 11–17
professional success, impact of
relationships on, 3–4
public conversations, 65, 78

Q

questions
that get answers, 52–58
that shut down people, 52–53
Quiet Quinn, conversational style
of, 68

R

rapport conversations, 7–8
real conversations, elements of,
12–13
relationships
benefits of, xii
extended reach of, 4–6
having conversations that
strengthen and heal
relationships, 100–102
impact of, 1–4
impact of on academic
success, 3–4
impact of on community
success, 4–6
impact of on mental
health, 2–3

impact of on organizational
  success, 4–6
impact of on physical
  health, 1–2
impact of on professional
  success, 3–4
impact of on self-esteem, 3
making of a top priority, 104
personal relationships, 15–16,
  17, 41
success as tied up with, 103
report conversations, 7–8, 9
respect
  choosing of, 37–39
  defined, 45
  importance of, 45–46
response, choosing how to control,
  31–34
Risk-avoider Ruth, conversational
  style of, 68
Risk-taker Rita, conversational style
  of, 68
Roseto, Pennsylvania, 5

S

saying no, 32
self-esteem, impact of relationships
  on, 3
Shakespeare, William, x
Sheri (case study), 48
silence, as element of real
  conversations, 13
small talk, importance of, x, 18
solutions, creation of, 79–102,
  107–108
speaking
  in difficult situations, 76–77
  practicing thinking before, 32

Step Away, as step to being
  successful, 94, 95–96
Step Back, as step to being
  successful, 94, 95
Step Up, as step to being
  successful, 94
storytelling, 6–11, 109
style
  communication of, 62–63
  complementary style, 74–76
  conversational style, 61, 63,
    65–68, 69, 71, 75, 78
  exploration of, 106–107
  natural styles, 67, 72–74
  ways style can work for you,
    74–78
  when conversations go wrong,
    often a matter of, 69–72
  why people don't get you,
    64–65
success
  impact of relationships on, 3–6
  listening and understanding
    your way to, 43–60,
    105–106
  taking steps to be successful,
    94–96
  that matters most, 18–19
  as tied up with
    relationships, 103
Susan Scott, 11

T

Talkative Tony, conversational style
  of, 68
Tannen, Deborah, 7, 12, 61, 103
technology, impact of on
  conversation, 8–11, 14

test cases
    Cassandra, 83, 84
    Connor, 82, 83
    Ellie, 82–84
text message, 9, 10, 14, 21, 22, 23,
        73, 104
thinking, practicing of before
        speaking, 32
Thoreau, Henry David, 43
Tonya (case study), 66–67
tough conversations, 39–40, 79–81,
        83, 84, 85, 86–90, 93, 94,
        95, 96, 97, 98, 99, 100,
        107, 108
triggers, 108
trust, building of, 17, 49

U

understanding, as way to success,
        43–60, 105–106

V

validation, listening as, 49
Vanzant, Iyanla, 79

W

wants
    people talking because they
        want something, 46–48
    tips to help you figure out what
        someone wants, 47
what comes next, taking
        responsibility for, 97–98
What's Up, Doc? (movie), 99
Winfrey, Oprah, 1

Printed in the United States
By Bookmasters